AF660952

ERNEST HEMINGWAY
The Turning Point

Dr. SATYABRATA DAS

ATLANTIC PUBLISHERS AND DISTRIBUTORS

Published by
ATLANTIC PUBLISHERS AND DISTRIBUTORS
B-2, Vishal Enclave, New Delhi-110 027
Phones 5413460, 5429987

Sales Office
4346/4C, Ansari Road, Darya Ganj,
New Delhi-110 002
Phones 3273880, 3285873
Fax 91-11-3285873

Copyright © The Publishers, 1996

ISBN 81-7156-440-2

No part of this book may be reproduced in any form without permission from the publisher except for the quotation of brief passages in criticism

Typeset at
APD Computer Graphics, Delhi

Printed in India at
Mehra Offset Printers, Delhi

Contents

Dedication

Dedicated to my dear parents whose love, care and blessings made me a *man*.

Preface

The influence of the Spanish Civil War was enormous and far-reaching on Hemingway. It brought about a complete reorientation of his approach to life that was marked by a change at the thematic and the stylistic level of his writings. This is quite visible and conspicuous from Nick Adams to Robert Jordan through Jake Barnes, Frederic Henry and Harry Morgan. The transformation is clear and promising: from Nada and nihilism to affirmation, from defeatism to conviction, from despair to optimism and, above all, from atomic individualism to social commitment and universal brotherhood. This study makes an effort to focus on these unexplored dimensions of Hemingway's art and personality.

SATYABRATA DAS

ABBREVIATIONS

The following abbreviations are used for the titles in the reference:

AMF — *A Moveable Feast*
ARIT — *Across the River and Into the Trees*
DIA — *Death in the Afternoon*
AFTA — *A Farewell to Arms*
FWBT — *For Whom the Bell Tolls*
GHA — *The Green Hills of Africa*
IOT — *In Our Time*
NAS — *Nick Adams Stories*
OMAS — *The Old Man And the Sea*
MWW — *Men Without Women*
SAR — *The Sun Also Rises*
THAHN — *To Have And Have Not*
WTN — *Winner Takes Nothing*
First 49 — *The Fifth Column and the First Forty-nine Stories*

INTRODUCTION

Hemingway and the Spanish Civil War: A Turning Point :

The failure of the Spanish Civil War, the defeat of the Republican Spanish army left most of the intellectuals, who were involved in the cause, disillusioned and cynical. But among the very few, who survived the wave and sublimated the shock, Hemingway was one.

The Spanish Civil War which Hemingway initially joined as an anti-war-propagandist eventually became a turning point in his life and writings. This book is an insightful study of the life and works of Hemingway in the Spanish Civil War perspective. This study shows how his early writings (pre-Spanish Civil War) are visibly marked by the shock of his wounding in the World War I that gave a nagging anxiety and dread for death, darkness and misfortune to all his early protagonists from Nick Adams to Capt. Frederic Henry (*A Farewell to Arms*). Hemingway, himself, was in no better circumstances either. He struggled really hard to ward off his dread for darkness and death that partly explains his craze for bullfighting and big game hunting. But, despite his best efforts, there was no let off till, of course, he went to the Spanish Civil War. It was Hemingway's exposure to the Spanish Civil War atmosphere that possibly acted therapeutically, and his chronic anxiety and insomnia syndrome give way finally. Correspondingly, all his later (post-Spanish Civil War) protagonists never show any sign of diffidence or defeatism thereafter. Interestingly, the concluding part of his novel *To Have and Have Not*, which he changed after his first visit to the Spanish Civil War (the evidence is clear and strong in the manuscript which this author examined in the U.S.A.), marks the beginning of the change that becomes more and more conspicuous in the subsequent works, such as, *For Whom the Bell Tolls* and *The Old Man and the Sea*. Besides, a corresponding and remarkable change commences in the theme and the narrative perspective of Hemingway hereafter.

CHAPTER I
FROM "I" TO "WE"

This study is an attempt at examining the major works of Ernest Hemingway in the broad Spanish Civil War perspective. The whole dialectic is based upon three fundamental hypotheses:

Firstly, Hemingway's works, as reflected in his protagonists' approach to life, show a pattern of steady evolution.

Secondly, 'Life', as they demonstrate it, is inherently painful and tragic. Besides, they offer no illusion that an individual can ever escape the harsh reality of life, however, hard one may try.

Finally, with this thwarted vision of life the protagonists of Hemingway, in the course of their journey, continually look forward to a sort of life that must be meaningful and worth living.

On the basis of the above hypotheses, this study takes a fresh look at the major writings of Hemingway to find out whether the Spanish Civil War did really serve as the main source of inspiration for the protagonist to rise above his hitherto narrow atomic individuality to reach out to a broad global vision of life, a meaningful pattern in life.

In view of the profusion of critical responses to Hemingway, it seems necessary to specify at the beginning the proposed approach of this study.

As a matter of fact, there has been a great consensus of criticism on the autobiographical overtones of Hemingway's writings. To mention a few, major critics like Philip Young, Sheridan Baker, Granville Hicks and Earl Rovit have drawn biographical parallels extensively to connect various incidents and plots of Hemingway's fictional writings with his own real life experiences. Philip Young, who makes a psycho-analytical (Freudian) approach, takes

Hemingway's wounding on the Italian front (during World War I) as the central clue to his treatment of Hemingway's works. Hemingway's obsession with the themes of violence, pain and death, as Young looks at them, was mainly due to his wound that left a lasting scar on his body and his mind as well. His fictional writings, therefore, reflect the writer's life-long struggle to purge himself of his terrible obsession and trauma. Further, on the basis of Hemingway's changing response to life, Young brings forth a division in the line of his protagonists, the Hemingway hero and the code-hero. While the former type is a thinly disguised autobiographical figure, "the generic Nick", who keeps changing his age and experience through Jake Barnes, Frederic Henry, Robert Jordan and Richard Cantwell, the latter type is a comparatively simple and liberated one (36-38).

Earl Rovit, on the other hand, treats this prototype Nick Adams as *Tyro* and the Code-heroes as *Tutors* (55). Rovit's classification corresponds to Young's to a great extent, though his approach is not psycho-analytical.

Long before Philip Young or Earl Rovit gave their interpretations of Hemingway's writings, Granville Hicks, in his book *The Great Tradition*, had made a profound and influential statement on Hemingway:

> Hemingway has, as a matter of fact, two heroes: the autobiographical. . . and the hero that Hemingway is not but thinks he would like to be (274).

Sheridan Baker finds evidence of autobiographical elements in Hemingway's writings. In the context of Robert Jordan, in *For Whom the Bell Tolls*, he observes:

> Jordan is, of course, Hemingway again, with a father who has committed suicide and a grand-father he admires (112).

Carlos Baker, another major Hemingway critic and biographer, however, does not subscribe to the biographical interpretation of Hemingway's works. As he makes it clear in the introduction to his book *Hemingway: The Writer as Artist*, he does not intend to write about "the private battles or his public wars" (xiii). On the other hand, Prof. Baker chooses to reveal "a substructure of symbolic meanings which has gone unrecorded and for the most part unobserved" (xiv).

Yet another comparatively recent finding of a scholar seems to counter effectively the biographical approach to Hemingway's writings. In the course of analyzing two of the artist's much discussed and highly acknowledged autobiographical short stories, "In Another Country" and "Now I Lay Me", James Steinke asserts that these stories are not really a fictionalized history of Hemingway at all. To substantiate his point against the tremendous force of biographical criticism, Steinke (1985) quotes Hemingway from one of his hand-written manuscripts presently preserved in John F. Kennedy Library, Boston. As a matter of fact, Hemingway seems to have written that piece as a perspective chapter for *A Moveable Feast* to clarify the relationship between art and his own experience under the title "On writing in the first-person" which begins with the writer's caution against the possible mistake of looking at his work as fictionalized personal history:

> When you first start writing stories in the first person, if the stories are made so real that people believe them, the people reading them nearly always think the stories really happened to you (Item 179 a-1) (32-39).

The objective of this study, however, is not to examine Hemingway's writings in terms of either hero and code-hero or *Tyro* and *Tutor* or autobiographical works and objective works. The focal-point of this study is, on the other hand, intended to be Hemingway's major works to bring home the point that the Spanish Civil War was truly a turning point in Hemingway's writings. This study proposes to examine Hemingway's major writings against the backdrop of the Spanish Civil War writings of Hemingway *vis-a-vis* his post-Spanish Civil War writings. If one traces the evolution of Hemingway's writings there emerges a clear pattern. At the beginning comes Nick Adams, the young adventurer in the Michigan Wood. Nick is the central character of *In Our Time*, the first major publication of Hemingway, that came out in 1925 with fifteen stories and a series of vignettes alternating with the stories. In two other subsequent short story collections, *Men Without Women* (1927) and *Winner Takes Nothing* (1933), Nick continues to be the central character of most of the stories.

As the stories clearly reveal, this young protagonist Nick Adams is a highly sensitive boy who, in the course of his various experiences with situations in life, discovers that violence, pain and brutality are an inalienable part of life. Commenting on Nick Adams, Philip Young writes:

> Here is a boy, after that a man, who both in his early environment and later out on his own has been coming in contact with "life" in our time (26).

And each bit of these experiences for Nick Adams has been in some way "violent, evil or unsettling"(26) for which there is no answer available to Nick. Joseph De Falco too observes that Hemingway's hero essentially projects the disillusionments of the modern man in "his struggle to come to terms with a world he cannot truly understand" (2).

II

Nick Adams, the young Hemingway protagonist, who begins his long journey of life from his very adolescence, is exposed to life's brutalities quite early. Nick's first hand experience of violence and death is shown in stories like "Indian Camp", "The Doctor and the Doctor's Wife", "The Battler", and "The Killers".

In the story, "Indian Camp", the young innocent Nick Adams is exposed to his first ever experience with the inherent violence, death and tragedy in human life. Nick, the son of a doctor, accompanies his father on one of his visits to an Indian family where his father carries on a caesarean operation without anaesthesia. The child is safely brought out, but the poor Indian husband, unable to stand his wife's agony, cuts his throat with a razor and dies. Nick, hardly in his adolescence now, witnesses this harsh reality of life, and thus his initiation into the darker aspects of life starts. On their way back, Nick keeps putting many fundamental questions relating to life and its mysteries to his father:

"Why did he kill himself, Daddy?"

"Do many men kill themselves, Daddy?"

"Is dying hard?" (*IOT*, 21).

Such experience of horror and violence shocks Nick Adams though the effect is temporary. It is because of Nick's immature mind that fails to respond to such experience consciously. De Falco very rightly points out Nick's state of mind when he observes: "His actions and responses are unemotive and childlike" (40).

But ironically, two dominant feelings occupy Nick Adams soon after he is out of the Indian Camp. Firstly, in the protective arms of his loving father he feels completely secure. Secondly, he has a queer feeling of "immortality" — the illusion that almost persists with Nick Adams till he is gravely wounded in the war later.

The feeling of absolute security in the protective care of his father that Nick Adams has is abruptly shaken in the story, "The Doctor and the Doctor's Wife". In the story, there is the scene of a brief altercation between Nick's father and a giant like Indian, Dick Boulton. The scene of altercation is very brief, but it is charged with high tension, particularly the manner in which Dick intimidates the Doctor and the latter's visible embarrassment and demoralization, that leaves young Nick shocked and bewildered. This experience of Nick rudely shatters his implicit faith in the parental protection and the security of home. When Nick finds to his horror that his father, whom he had been looking upon as his protector, is vulnerable himself, his illusion about the parental protection is lost. And Nick suddenly finds himself almost in the street, as his home is no more a sanctuary for him.

Thus, Nick's journey that begins with "Indian Camp" passes through his recurring encounter with the stark reality of life, and the cumulative effects of such experience on his mind leaves him unsettled, and deeply disturbed.

The feeling of vulnerability and insecurity even at home leads to a feeling of alienation in Nick that will be further reinforced after he is wounded at Fossalta in war.

In the chain of events that mark the education of the Hemingway protagonist in a world of violence and tragedy, there comes "The Battler". In the course of one of his adventures Nick Adams runs into the camp of an ex-boxing champion, Ad Francis, who is now crazy and without form.

"I am crazy," Ad Francis introduces himself. And continues, "When you got it you don't know about it" (*IOT*, 69).

Nick feels sick to see his badly mutilated face and is shocked to see this strange man introducing himself as Ad Francis and confessing that he is crazy. As the story moves, things pass smoothly and amicably in pretty good spirit. Nick, save his feeling of sickness at seeing the badly scarred face of Ad, feels otherwise comfortable. Suddenly Ad becomes silent. His silence had a mysterious horror about it that makes Nick nervous. Finally, Ad bursts out violently, first in a gush of words, followed by an attempt to maul Nick. Nick, quite unprepared for such a dramatic turn of events, is left almost dazed.

However, the situation is timely tackled by Ad's Negro mate, Bugs, who taps Ad on his head and puts him to rest. On Nick's request Bugs relates a very complex account of the sad life of Ad. He tells how Ad Francis was happy and affluent some years ago. He was in top form as a boxer and married the lady who was his manager and whom he loved. But the people around created all sorts of "unpleasantness"about it. The lady somehow resembled Ad for which they ascribed incest to their marriage and made their life miserable. Finally, the social pressure was so much that "they commenced to have disagreements, and one day she just went off and never came back". As Bugs added, "He was busting people all the time after she went away and they put him in jail" (*IOT*, 77).

Nick's initiation into violence and tragedy in human life as he comes across in "Indian Camp" is further complicated as he meets "The Battler". Here, the complexity of human mind and its dreadful dimensions unnerve Nick. The exposure to characters like Ad Francis makes Nick feel perplexed and confused.

In "The Killers" Nick encounters the threat to his life in much greater magnitude than in "The Battler". The atmosphere of "The Killers" is much more horrifying than that of "The Battler".

Commenting on the significance of the story, "The Killers", Joseph De Falco describes it as a "transition story"(63) that marks the development of the protagonist from his adolescence to manhood. As against the purely "unemotive"(De Falco, 40) response of young Nick to the situation of violence in "Indian Camp", "The Doctor and the Doctor's Wife" and "The Battler", in "The Killers" he acts emotionally. At the first confrontation with these forces of evil he wants to run away. This very attempt to run away sets Nick on his journey into the complexities of life. First, Nick tries to persuade Ole Anderson, the man whom the hoodlums wanted to kill that evening in the Bar. Nick, fresh and inexperienced in the world of violence, thinks that something could be done about Ole Anderson's impending tragedy. But Nick is taken aback, and cannot believe his own ears when Ole Anderson stoically says:

> "There isn't anything I can do about it."

The conversation that follows between Nick Adams and Ole Anderson is worth examining:

> "Don't you want me to go and see the police?" "No," Ole Anderson said. "That wouldn't do any good." "Isn't there something I could do?" "No. There isn't anything to do." . . .
> "Couldn't you get out of town?" "No," Ole Anderson said, "I'm through with all that running around" (*NAS*, 70).

In the story young Nick Adams is cast against two comparatively more experienced and mature characters, Ole Anderson and George. Ole Anderson, who is the victim and who may be killed any moment, takes the threat stoically for he realizes that nothing can possibly be done to prevent it. George, the bartender, too seems convinced about the hopelessness of the situation and believes that Ole Anderson will be killed. On the contrary, Nick Adams, who is yet to be fully introduced to the working of the cruel, irrational forces of the world, still has plenty of illusions about things. He keeps on proposing for some action, some attempt, to avert the tragedy. Finally, seeing no hope he gets thoroughly perplexed and says: "It's an awful thing ... I am going to get out of the town" (*NAS*, 69).

To Nick, the experience with "The Killers" is of much greater educative value than any of his previous experiences. When he is gagged by the two hoodlums, he thinks, "He had never had a towel in his mouth before" (*NAS*, 65). In this context, Cleanth Brooks and Robert Penn Warren observe that this story shows "the process of initiation, the discovery of evil and disorder, and the first step toward the mastery of the discipline" (Benson, 193). Jeseph De Falco comments thus:

> Ironically, Nick's final response to the whole affair, "I'm going to get out of this town", is the reflex of what Anderson has revealed to him in the previous dialectic of learning (70).

Whatever Nick Adams learns from the situation here is later manifested in the observation of Frederic Henry on life in *A Farewell to Arms*. Frederic Henry, failing in his attempt to make a "separate peace", realizes that an individual cannot run away and escape the persecution of the inevitable forces in life. The experience of Nick in "The Killers" is confirmed in two other stories, "The Battler" and "The Light of the World". Both the stories show the protagonist who is desperately trying to run away from the experiences of life. In "The Light of the World" Nick is exposed to the sordid complexities of life when he sees some prostitutes for the first time in his life.

In "The Killers", through his ordeal, Nick is shockingly introduced into the senseless, meaningless violence of the world, and realizes the fragility of human life. The experience has a great influence on Nick's life because he has no illusion hereafter that this world ensures any security to the individual. This sort of existential awareness that Nick develops is continually reinforced in the course of his recurring experience with such forces in life.

The killers who come to murder Ole Anderson in the story do not know him personally, nor do they have any vendetta to settle with him. They simply and casually want to kill him for the sake of somebody else. That such meaningless and casual brutality is a part of modern life, of "our time", Nick realizes through this experience. The same sort of horror, of course in a much greater magnitude, is enacted in Hemingway's later novel on the World War I, *A Farewell to Arms*. In that novel there is a scene that shows how, on vague charges, the officers in the army are shot down. And finally, Frederic Henry, finding no meaning in such senseless brutality and being completely disillusioned, runs away from the line. This tendency, however, is marked as early as in Nick when he meets the killers and fails to arouse Ole Anderson to action:

> "It's a hell of a thing."
>
> "It's a hell of a thing."
>
> "It's an awful thing" (*MWW*, 69).

As Joseph M. Flora very accurately perceives, four times in "The Killers" Hemingway reminds us of the darkness in the world out there, "a world badly in need of a little light" (97). When Nick Adams longs for a "little light" to get out of the dark abyss, the baffling complexities of life, he again finds himself in a greater whirlpool of violence and senseless killing before he is aware of it. As Joseph M. Flora observes:

> The most traumatic of Nick's experiences are those he had as a soldier, especially the trial of battle and his wounding in battle (105).

III

Presently the Hemingway protagonist joins the Great War with the usual youthful ideal and enthusiasm. But the euphoria is shattered in no time when he is gravely wounded in the war, and is thrown out with a wounded body and a wrecked mind. Hemingway recreates this typical psychology of the youth in his introduction to *Men at War* later in 1942:

> When you go to war as a boy you have a great illusion of immortality. Other people can get killed, not you... . Then when you are badly wounded the first time you lose that illusion and you know it can happen to you (7).

As a matter of fact, till the moment of wounding death seemed to be a mere abstraction to him. Now suddenly it becomes a frightening, terrifying reality that gave him, as Malcolm Cowley (1962) calls, "nightmares at noonday" (Weeks, 41). We may recall Nick Adams' journey back from the "Indian Camp" with his father in the boat. When the first day-light brightens the lake, Nick, in the protective arms of his father in the boat, "felt quite sure that he would never die" (*IOT*, 21). Nick refuses to accept the horrors of pain and death that he has just witnessed in the Indian Camp. And he has a strange feeling or illusion of immortality that persists with him through his harrowing experiences with "The Battler", "The Killers" till of course he is wounded finally in the war. With the war-wound Hemingway's protagonist completes the first phase of his evolution toward the ultimate realization of the truth in life. Of course, he reaches this point quite unwittingly, without any conscious attempt. And for this progress of Nick's education in the world, as Hemingway mentions later in the course of *Green Hills of Africa*, war was a "great advantage"(108), although apparently the experience appeared to be the end of all.

The protagonist, as such, comes out of the war physically wounded and morally broke. Here, the Hemingway protagonist was not the case of an individual alone. He represented a whole generation of post-war youth for whom the world would never be the same again. The First World War shattered the dreams and faith of the individual, that he had for centuries, about his tradition and his social institutions. He suddenly found himself thrown out of home, out of society, as though the very umbilical-cord between the individual and the society is snapped with violence. As Clinton S. Burhans, Jr. (1968) rightly observes, this war-worn, disoriented protagonist "finds himself isolated and a stranger''(322). The physical wound, however, healed up soon. But the shock of it continued to haunt for a long time. As Joseph M. Flora asserts, "The most traumatic of Nick's experiences are those he had as a soldier..."(97).

This study aims at demonstrating that the Hemingway protagonist passes through these phases of violence, horror and disillusionment, and finally finds the light he has been longing for all his life.

Through a series of provocative stories such as, "Soldier's Home", "Now I Lay Me", "The Way You'll Never Be" and "In Another Country", and many others, Hemingway conducts us like a tourist guide into the bitter conflicts, despair and disillusionment of the protagonist who is just out of the war. All these stories have a general atmosphere of conflict, despair, disillusionment, sentimentality, inaction, purposelessness and above all, an acute feeling of utter futility, of nothingness, *Nada*. But eventually, this damned protagonist gets out of this veritable hell, and attains the desired equilibrium, stability and the spiritual regeneration that dispel the irrevocable darkness with its surge of fresh bright light.

Now we shall look into the life and predicament of the new war-worn, war-torn protagonist who is just back home after his nightmarish encounter with death on the battlefield. As this soldier returns home, we find him much sobered, but a deeply disillusioned man. Though he is given a hero's reception he has a feeling of great uneasiness as he fails to adjust himself to a society based on some hollow, sham values. As we watch Krebs in "Soldier's Home", he feels "angry", "sick and vaguely nauseated"(*IOT*, 7). The concept of home as a place of love, comfort and security appears like a fiction to Krebs. As Roger Asselineau aptly remarks:

> The bottom seemed to have dropped out of everything. The world was empty, life absurd and meaningless". . . (142).

The protagonist seems to be totally drained out spiritually. Love, the very sustaining force behind human existence, seems to have dried up in his breast. As we see in the case of Krebs ("Soldier's Home") or lady Brett Ashley and Jake Barnes later in *The Sun Also Rises*, the very source seems to have dried up. They seem to have been sapped of this sustaining emotion; hence the tragedy. As the case of Krebs shows, he is not even able to respond to his mother's repeated appeal for love:

> "Don't you love your mother — dear boy?"
> Krebs replies curtly: "No" and he adds: "I don't love anybody" (*IOT*, 7).

As Nakajima rightly observes, "The title of the Soldier's Home is ironical, for the home repels the soldier"(27).

Again, this wounded protagonist of Hemingway constantly complains about his phobia for darkness, and fails to get a sleep in the night:

> I myself did not want to sleep because I had been living for a long time with the knowledge that if I ever shut my eyes in the dark and let myself go, my soul would go out of my body (*NAS*, 144).

And he too seems to remember the cause:

> I had been that way for a long time, ever since I had been blown up at night and felt it go out of me and go off and then come back (*NAS*, 144).

Thus the young protagonist of Hemingway is tormented by a deep trauma which the war-wound has left in his psyche. He has a morbid fear that if he ever shut his eyes in the dark his soul would go out of his body.

As Kenneth G. Johnson (1971) believes:

> Nick's 'great awakening' has been a nightmarish, traumatic experience which has left him psychically wounded (9).

The protagonist who is now in bed, in a state of convalescence, is mostly wide awake all through the night since the moment he received the mortar-wound. Arthur Waldhorn points out:

> At the instant of his wound, Nick (like Frederic Henry in *A Farewell to Arms*) had felt his soul leave his body. Since then, the threshold of sleep seems an abyss of terror, a place where self is lost for ever (63).

Thus, right from the moment he receives the mortar-wound on the battlefield he develops an acute insomnia, a phobia for darkness and, the worst of all, a high-sensitiveness, which is a clear sign of neurosis. In the quiet hours of the night even the feeble sound of the 'silkworms feeding' horrifies him. As De Falco observes, the sound of the feeding silkworms are like "the Greek Chorus reminding man of his inescapable fate" (112). In other words, the Hemingway-protagonist seems to have become acutely aware of the uncertainty, insecurity, vulnerability and, above all, the inevitability of fate. He realizes the grave limitation of the individual who has to bear with the assaults of fate, however, painful or agonizing they may be. This very tragic awareness tends to make the protagonist edgy, jittery and neurotic. And the reversal comes so abruptly that he scarcely gets any time to get reconciled to it. Thus his feelings tend to be intensely nihilistic, questioning his manhood every now and then.

According to Earl Rovit's findings, the protagonist in the story "Now I Lay Me" is in his convalescence after he is wounded (1927) at Fossalta, and suffers from a sort of "Proustian inability to go to sleep", for he has a great foreboding that if he sleeps in the dark "that might carry him over the thin edge" (Rovit,70).

The thin edge really matters because at the moment of wounding, the protagonist had a strange awareness of the twilight, between consciousness and unconsciousness, which keenly resembled the thin veil between Life and Death.

This Proustian Syndrome that denies sleep to this war-worn protagonist of Hemingway continues to torment him even after he is released from the hospital with his wound clinically healed up. In "A Way You'll Never Be" (1933), the protagonist is seen coming back to resume his duty in his outfit. But as Rovit rightly observes, "His nerves are shattered and his mind has a tendency to jump around and off, as though its flywheel were disconnected" (80).

Thus it is the war and its wound that seem to make all the difference for this young protagonist of Hemingway. Though the physical wound is healed up the trauma persists. In spite of all his efforts the protagonist just cannot get over his feeling of insecurity and nothingness. In his desperate bid to ward off insomnia and acute fear and restlessness the protagonist tries to gather himself up by reminiscing all his past happy experiences. Mostly he would try to keep himself engaged with his memories of fishing in all vivid detail. Even this is not possible always:

> But some nights I could not fish, and on those nights I was cold-awake and said my prayers over and over and tried to pray for all the people I had ever known (*NAS*, 146).

Such a desperate, involuntary act of the protagonist to identify himself with the larger humanity certainly helps him consolidate his self that is under great threat. As Carlos Baker comments on the miserable state of Hemingway's mind before he went to Spain to report on the Civil War:

> Premonitions of possible death struck him periodically like twinges of rheumatism (*A Life Story,* 445).

As we observe, the desperate attempts of the protagonist at consolidating his own self to overcome the threat, the insomnia and the *Nada*, do not succeed until *For Whom the Bell Tolls*, where Robert Jordan realizes it finally.

As De Falco comments on the misery of the Hemingway protagonist during this phase of his journey:

> He is the picture of the traditional wounded hero languishing in the night-world unable to reach the source of the healing, redemptive power (113).

The next story with the same war-worn, traumatized protagonist, "A Way You'll Never Be", is based on the theme of alienation, nihilism and insomnia. De Falco again shows the subtle tension that sustains the story all along. He sums up the story as "the tale of an individual who is poised on the borderline of sanity and insanity, reality and unreality and ultimately, life and death" (115).

The main difference between this story and "Now I Lay Me" is that, while in "Now I Lay Me" he was all the time in bed, trying to ward off the horror of existence with his wakeful dream, in "A Way You'll Never Be" he is out of his bed but continues to be haunted all the while. Besides, "Now I Lay Me" is mostly cast in the night while "A Way You'll Never Be" is cast in broad daylight, under the afternoon Sun.

The story begins with Nicholas Adams going on a bicycle across a recently abandoned army post. He passes by the dead bodies of soldiers whose pockets are out and flies are swarming on them. The purpose of Nick's visit to the front post is not known at the beginning. In the course of his talk with the Captain, he says: "I am demonstrating the American Uniform" (*NAS*, 163); and he further makes it clear that he is now "reformed out of the war" (163).

But, in spite of his best efforts to show that he is perfectly all right, his troubled psyche is exposed at some unguarded moments. When the Captain asks him about his wounding, he says:

> I'm all right. I can't sleep without a light of some sort. That's all I have now (*NAS*, 159).

Thus, the insomnia, the fear of the darkness, still continues to bother Nick. Again, while speaking to an adjutant about the expected arrival of several millions of Americans, Nick reveals his inner wound. Though there is an apparent enthusiasm in his speech the inner-wound lurks behind. Nick eagerly announces:

> Americans twice as large as myself, healthy, with clean hearts, sleep at night, never been wounded, never been blown up, never had their heads caved in, never scared . . . (162).

The above passage unmistakably reveals the deep trauma that Nick still has, which he is desperately striving to ward off. He again confesses that he is strangely scared of a particular vision of a long yellow house and a different width of the river (162). Its implication becomes clear, as Philip Young observes correctly, after almost twenty years in *Across the River and Into the Trees*. This scene recurs there which presently comes very often to Nick and then it becomes clear that "this is the place where he was wounded" (Young, 25).

The same traumatized, high-strung protagonist appears again in the story, "In Another Country", and says:

> I was very much afraid to die, and often lay in bed at night by myself, wondering how I would be when I went back to the front again (*NAS*, 171).

Here, the acute awareness of Death is more conspicuous than in any other story of this period.

Secondly, the protagonist (a wounded Major who is convalescing presently)shows his strong antipathy to marriage, for he has recently lost his young wife in pneumonia. This very fact is symptomatic of Frederic Henry in *A Farewell to Arms*. When, by the way, the question of marriage arises (in the context of the narrator) the Major reacts vehemently, rather hysterically:

> "A man must not marry."

And he continues:

> If he is to lose everything, he should not place himself in a position to lose that. He should not place himself in a position to lose. He should find things he cannot lose (*NAS*, 172-73).

The point worth noting in this story is that in spite of the long ordeal which the protagonist has passed through, he is still left with some illusion that an individual probably, if cautious and guarded enough, can save something from being ruined. That very illusion, however, will get shattered at the end of *A Farewell to Arms* when Frederic Henry, despite all his efforts and care, fails to save what he loves most.

As Ray B. West Jr. (1962) rightly points out, the first three important works of Hemingway (*In Our Time* , *The Sun Also Rises* and *A Farewell to Arms*) deal with the same theme: "the condition of man in a society upset by the violence of war"(28). To put it more directly, these stories and the early novels show the victimization of the individual in a violent war-worn world.

The first novel that brought fame and recognition to Hemingway, *The Sun Also Rises*, is an extension of the theme of "violence and the predicament of the individual" that marked the stories of *In Our Time*. Commenting on this book James T. Farrell (1962) calls it "the definitive account of a war-wearied lost generation" (4).

A look at the above analysis of Henry makes the inherent quest of the Hemingway protagonist clear. As Jake Barnes ruminates:

> All I wanted to know was how to live in it. May be if you found out how to live in it, you learned from that what it was all about (*SAR*, 148).

The same problem that troubled Jake Barnes keeps bothering Frederic too. He is yet to find the truth that Jake sought all his life for. In fact the quest continues right from the very beginning when young Nick Adams asks his father the fundamental questions concerning life, on their way back from the Indian Camp:

> "Why did he kill himself, Daddy?" "Do many men kill themselves, Daddy?" "Is dying hard?" and so on (*IOT*, 21).

Thus Nick Adams, the innocent boy, who confronts the sinister forces of life, is instinctively motivated to look for a viable rationale, a meaningful pattern, that could possibly sustain the individual in the face of a cruel, hostile world.

What is to be one's rationale, one's code of conduct in a world full of pain, violence and death? This quest for realizing the basic truth in life keeps the Hemingway protagonist occupied all along till Harry Morgan, of course, visualizes the first glimpse of it just before his death. Till that moment, as Sheridan Baker rightly observes, the Hemingway protagonist found this world "cruel, whimsical, senseless and with no meaning nor plan" (2). Thus as both Philip Young and Sheridan Baker find, they remain perpetually in a "Dover Beach" atmosphere. They find neither joy, nor love, nor light, nor certitude, nor peace" (Young, 245).

The atmosphere of the Nick Adams stories, the interchapters of *In Our Time*, *The Sun Also Rises, A Farewell to Arms* and *To Have And Have Not* remain largely gloomy, complex and horrifying that rightly prompted Malcolm Cowley (1962) to comment that the Hemingway protagonist sees "nightmare at noonday"(Weeks, 41).

V

As we have already noted, Nick Adams is too young to probe into the mysteries of life. He is just a passive participant in the experiences of life without any conscious reaction to it. All his actions, therefore, are purely biological or instinctive, or "unemotive", as De Falco affirms (40).

Jake Barnes, the war-worn protagonist of *The Sun Also Rises*, painfully realizes the dreadful agony of life, passes through endless nights without sleep, but lacks adequate insight and reason to see through the puzzling issues of life in a proper perspective. He is, thus, all along confused and behaves as an impotent weakling that provokes Robert Cohn to call him a "bloody pimp" when Lady Brett slips into other men's arms right under his very nose (*SAR*, 197).

Jake, therefore, cannot be called a man proper, for he does not seem to have the minimum self-confidence, or will-power. He only sees things happening to him, he groans in pain, he whimpers helplessly; but he makes no effort to get away from it, or to reason out or to rationalize the situation to lessen the suffering. All his reactions are purely sentimental, hence ineffectual. He loves Brett, longs for her company, but fails to consummate. When Brett goes out with her male friends, Jake cries and swears helplessly:

> To hell with Brett. To hell with you lady Ashley (*SAR*, 30).

But he cannot forget or forsake the woman who torments him so much. Thus, till the very end, Jake sees no hope, no meaning in life. He remains basically an extension of Nick Adams's personality. But while Nick Adams enjoyed the bliss of innocence and could remain mostly untouched by the complexities of the world, Jake is fully and consciously aware of them, becomes directly a party to the complexities of life for his sentimental doting on a nymphomaniac who torments him every moment. When Jake comes away dejected to France, leaving Brett in Pamplona with the bullfighter Pedro Romero, he soon gets a wire from her and reflects:

> That was it. Send a girl off with one man. Introduce

> her to another to go off with him. Now go and bring her back. And sign the wire with love (*SAR*, 250).

This interior monologue of Jake is greatly ironical and revealing of his inner conflict, his tragedy. Thus he largely remains a weak-kneed "damned pimp", as Cohn rightly accuses him (*SAR*, 197).

But with Frederic Henry the case is much better. Though Frederic never sees the light in his life time, he is remarkably more advanced in his quest and thus comes closer to his goal than Jake Barnes.

Primarily, Frederic is not damned with inaction and thoughtlessness like Jake. He is a man of action. Besides, Henry is comparatively much more clear in his head, and reasons out the baffling complexities of life, and thus approaches closely the final point in this quest.

Catherine shows great courage and conviction in every act of her life and finally passes away fighting. Her courage and her confidence, somehow, give a sort of premonition to Henry. Henry has seen more of life, gone deeper into the savage reality of life. Thus through his own understanding of life he reflects:

> If people bring so much courage to this world the world has to kill them to break them (*AFTA*, 258).

This sort of analysis and observation shows the sharpness and clarity of reason which his predecessors, Jake Barnes and Nick Adams, did not have. Nick, of course, is excusable for he is too young to reflect on the complex issues of life. But Jake Barnes is a clear case of despondency and inaction that impaired his thought process too. Compared to him, Frederic Henry shows great control over his situation, decisiveness, alertness of mind and power of reason. The way he escapes the imminent shooting, and the courage he shows in swimming across a river in spate, and ferrying Catherine across to Switzerland in a stormy night, cannot be thought of in respect of Jake Barnes. As Waldhorn very rightly points out:

> Sterility haunts Jake Barnes's wasteland, fear the shadowy recesses of Nick Adam's world (115).

And on Frederic Henry, Waldhorn comments:

> At the center of that small world stands Hemingway's representative man, an apprentice learning to endure the tragic conditions of life, questioning some foundation to support a belief beyond *Nada* (Waldhorn, 118).

But finally, with all his positive aspects and promising traits Frederic Henry fails to reach the point, the source of light, at the far end of the dark tunnel. When he finds no pattern in the inevitable tragedy that strikes him, he remembers one of his own experiences that suits as the finest analogy to an individual's predicament in this world:

> Once in a camp I put a log on top of the fire and it was full of ants. As it commenced to burn, the ants swarmed out and went first toward the center where the fire was; then turned back and ran toward the end. When there were enough on the end they fell off into the fire. Some got out, their bodies burnt and flattened and went off not knowing where they were going. But most of them went toward the fire and then back toward the end and swarmed on the cool end and finally fell off into the fire (*AFTA*, 338).

The above parallelism is, indeed, apt and befitting. It reminds one of man's inevitable fate. A man may attempt to break away, to defy, and to opt for a separate peace. But he cannot escape the ultimate tragic reality, Death. This truth is effectively dramatized in the life and exploits of Lt. Frederic Henry in *A Farewell to Arms*. It reminds one of Gloucester's words in *King Lear*:

> As flies to wanton boys, are we to the Gods. (IV, I 36-37) (Arden Shakespeare, 149).

One thing worth noting at this point is that all through those early works, despite their subtle difference in their approach to life, and their responses to the various situations, all of them share one common trait. Even Harry Morgan too has that aspect in common with them. That is their unmistakable concern for "self". Whatever they think or attempt to do is clearly directed to some gratification of their own interest. In spite of their education through life and their maturity of vision they fail to rise above their self, which alone can help them realize the ultimate truth in life, the real secret of existence, of a meaningful survival. This very flaw, however, Harry Morgan realizes just on the eve of his death.

VI

As the pattern emerges from the preceding discussion, an important common feature with all the early Hemingway protagonists is their atomic self-concern, their narrow individualistic approach to life in terms of their own pleasure or well-being. As Harold Bloom observes on Hemingway:

> He is an elegiac poet who mourns the self, who celebrates the self. . . and who suffers division in the self (2-3).

This tendency of pursuing the self and eventually getting thwarted in the pursuit continues with these early protagonists of Hemingway well up to Harry Morgan. Harry, the central character of *To Have And Have Not*, all his life, is only concerned about the well-being of his tiny family. Having found his income inadequate in a fair endeavour he is tempted to switch over to a more lucrative, but highly illegal trafficking of contraband liquor. In the process he loses one of his arms. But even then he does not realize the limitation of his vision of life and continues to be on the look out for such lucrative business. His last trip turns out to be fatal, and brings an untimely end to Harry's life and pursuit, leaving his dependent family members to their own fate. Harry, despite his narrow self-concern like all his predecessors (such as, Nick, Jake and Henry), has another big plus point with him. First of all, he is much superior to Nick and Jake in will power, patience and courage to face the cruelty of life. He is again decidedly better than his immediate predecessor, Frederic Henry, in that he does not run away from life; he faces it in all its monstrosity and dies in the process. And one thing noble that he accomplishes is killing the extremists, the anti-socials whom he considers to be dangerous and detrimental to society. This very act, even at the fag-end of his life, enables him to get a flicker of the ultimate truth that all his predecessors including himself had been looking forward to. Harry dies; but before his death he realizes the truth that can make the struggle and horror of human existence meaningful. The bitter truth of the blundering pursuit of his own, and all his predecessors, is expressed in the few broken syllables which Harry blurts out before he dies expressing the view that a man alone has no chance and there should be collective action. Thus, Carlos Baker, considering Harry as superior to all his associates, observes:

> Within the illusion provided by *To Have and Have Not*, Harry Morgan emerges as a heroic and morally indefatigable figure, standing out like a stoic statue above the heads of his associates, gifted with qualities and abilities and determinations to which none of his companions can lay equal claim (*Writer as Artist*, 222).

Harry Morgan's death which marks his liberation or fulfilment, very much like Macomber's on the eve of his death, is the turning point in the evolution of the Hemingway protagonist and his writing as well. As Edgar Johnson rightly points out, the post-war skepticism of all these Hemingway protagonists was more or less like Descartes's provisional doubt that served as "a stage preparatory to a new departure", as *tabula rasa*, on which to construct a truer and more harmonious conception of life (137).

Sheridan Baker, in his observation on Francis Macomber, finds him much closer to Harry Morgan, as he too "grows to manhood under fire a few moments before his violent death" (98).

Carlos Baker further highlights the significance of Harry Morgan's story and affirms that it directly looks forward to *For Whom the Bell Tolls*. As Baker vindicates: "In two respects, at least, the Morgan story looks forward to *For Whom the Bell Tolls*". Firstly, as he argues: "in the development of emotional intensity". And secondly, "in Hemingway's capacity for the enlargement of character to heroic proportions" (*Writer as Artist*, 222).

This moment of revelation that Harry finally reaches is preceded by a brief period of trial and experimentation by the Hemingway protagonists. The protagonist, as such, has been hopefully looking forward to a sort of liberation from his trauma and deep-seated nihilism through his identification with the three act tragedy of the Spanish bullfight ritual and the big-game hunting. The ritual of bullfight, though it helped him mitigate his trauma to some extent, could not help him transcend spiritually the real fear of death. The primitive Spanish ritual saw to the genuineness of it that could elevate this drama of death in an arena to the level of tragedy with its cathartic effect on the audience. But with the new breed of bulls, the bullfighter certainly fails to impress the audience as a hero. So later on, Hemingway was quite skeptical about a possible spiritual transcendence through bullfight. As Robert O'Stephens notes:

> By the time of the Spanish Civil War it had become clear to him that death was the true measurer of human qualities and while "death is still very badly organized in war", it is, in war, beyond human tampering (91).

Thus in *Green Hills of Africa*, Hemingway observes:

> I thought about Tolstoy and about what a great advantage and experience of war was to a writer (70).

He further writes:

> Civil War is the best war for a writer, the most complete (71).

And he continues:

> Writers are forged in injustice as a sword is forged (71).

It now becomes clear that being sorely disappointed with bull-fighting, Hemingway looked upon war, Civil War in particular, as a rich source of inspiration for an artist. So, when the Spanish Civil War broke out, Hemingway considered it as a rare opportunity, and promptly went there to study it from close quarters and to utilize it for creative purposes. In fact, his experience in the Spanish Civil War

which can twist him or break him in any manner or at any time it wishes.

But slowly Harry becomes bolder and more assertive and develops a social commitment. When Harry kills the Chinese, Mr. Sing, he unlike any of the earlier Hemingway protagonists justifies the act in the broader context of social responsibility. When Harry's mate asks him why he killed the Chinese, he replies unequivocally, "To keep from killing twelve other chinks" (55).

Thus by killing Mr. Sing Harry makes a new beginning. He shows his social commitment. On this point, as Carlos Baker observes, Harry rises to "heroic proportion", and thus anticipates Robert Jordan in *For Whom the Bell Tolls* (*Writer as Artist*, 222).

This note of "self-reversal" and this discovery of "Social-dependence" (Oldsey, 32) is yet another important development in Harry's progress towards his ultimate realization at the end.

In the final encounter, when the extremists gun down his friend Albert without any provocation, Harry has a brief dialogue within himself. And finally he resolves his conflict and empties his barrel on them. Then he feels as though:

> All the cold was gone around his heart and he had the old hollow, singing feeling (171).

On this stoic, cool operation, Laurence Broer rightly comments:

> No conflict, no indecision, nothing hereafter. Harry is calm, cool, stoically poised (85).

Besides, Harry, unlike all his predecessors, develops an admirable self-confidence. At a certain point, in the course of an intimate, informal chat with his wife, Harry asserts:

> I got confidence. That's the only thing I have got (126).

This 'confidence' is an important and a purely new trait in the freshly emerging new protagonist of Hemingway's later novels.

This self-confidence and stoicism are reflected in Harry's action when he is wounded while running contraband liquor.

Harry's stoicism and endurance are distinctly felt against his mate who breaks down wailing. Rather Harry tries to console him: "Take it easy" (75). This reminds one of Santiago, the old protagonist of *The Old Man and the Sea.*

Yet another significant development in Harry's personality and attitude to life is his ability for self-analysis and introspection. Like Santiago, he clearly analyses his blunder:

> I guess I bit off too much more than I could chew.
> I shouldn't have tried it (174).

This self-analysis of Harry is a clear step forward from all his predecessors and directly anticipates Santiago. Benson affirms that:

> With the death of Harry Morgan in *To Have And Have Not* comes the death of the early Hemingway protagonist (150).

And Carlos Baker finds in Harry Morgan the emergence of "a heroic and morally indefatigable figure, standing like a stoic statue" (*Writer as Artist*, 222), and Philip Young asserts that *To Have And Have Not* is a novel with a "message" (71).

And the message that this novel conveys is the result of a life-time quest. As Young writes:

> It is a death bed conversion; the words are Harry's last on earth: "No matter how a man alone ain't got no bloody f—ng chance" (71).

In the dying words of Harry there is indeed an unmistakable realization of a human solidarity and inter-dependence which finally culminates in *For Whom the Bell Tolls*. Edgar Johnson thinks that Harry Morgan "has been beaten up", because he tried "to fight alone" and this provides the "clue to victory" for all his heroes (140).

This transition that begins with Harry Morgan in *To Have And Have Not* culminates in *For Whom the Bell Tolls* later, and the trend continues through *Across the River and Into the Trees* and *The Old Man and the Sea*.

Commenting on this, Bernard Oldsey writes:

> Continuing where Harry Morgan left off, Robert Jordan and Anselmo constitute a further renunciation of lost-generation irresponsibility and negativism. For Jordan the world is still "worth fighting for" (33).

Then naturally the question follows, what possibly brought about such a dramatic, spectacular change in Hemingway's general approach to life which greatly affected his style and art too?

A careful study of Hemingway's life and his writings during the critical period of the thirties shows the drastic change that the writer went through between the early thirties and the late thirties which stretched into the early forties. This change shows how he almost moved from one extreme to the other.

Hemingway's two great non-fictional works, *Death in the Afternoon* and *The Green Hills of Africa*, give a clear account of the writer's indulgence in bullfighting and big-game hunting. As a matter of fact, in umpteen cases of this period, the journalistic and non-fictional pieces give clear evidence of Hemingway's passion for sensation and thrill. As he professes in one of the articles in *Esquire* (June 1935):

> Your correspondent's mind has been turned to shooting and he is inspired to offer this information on account of just having shot himself in the calves of both legs (*By-Line*, 199).

In the course of the same article, Hemingway makes an expert's observation on shooting, from a horse to a shark, and all sorts of big-game. This very piece of writing is greatly representative of Hemingway's craze for a life of sensation, thrill and adventure.

Again, in another piece in *Esquire* (April 1936), Hemingway writes:

> Certainly there is no hunting like the hunting of man and those who have hunted armed men long enough and liked it, never really care for anything else thereafter (*By-Line*, 236).

Thus, the above pieces of writing show Hemingway's way of life during this period. He was leading a boisterous and sensational life. And his attitude to people in general and the international issues of the time was narrow and parochial as it is clearly reflected in one of his articles in *Esquire*:

> No European country is our friend nor has been since the last war and no country but ones' own is worth fighting for (*By-Line*, 206).

The attitude of Hemingway, as it is reflected in these writings up to 1936, shows a clear continuation of *Death in the Afternoon* and *Green Hills of Africa*. And his highly parochial response to European issues, as can be seen in the passage quoted above, shows a continuation of Frederic Henry's disregard for common cause and his keenness for a separate peace. But, between the late 30s and early 40s Hemingway underwent a steady and rapid change, from a highly personal isolationism to a deep commitment to human solidarity, as the very title and the theme of *For Whom the Bell Tolls* show. Obviously, the Spanish Civil War brought about this transformation in Hemingway, from 'I' to 'We', from atomic self-centeredness to altruism. The stark contrast between the statement "no country but one's own is worth fighting for" and "No man is an Iland" (Donnes' epigraph for *FWBT*) is clearly realized.

But how could such a contradiction be resolved so easily and so soon? This very puzzle directs us to study Hemingway's participation in the Spanish Civil War and the surprising transformation that followed.

The final realization or "the death-bed conversion" of Harry Morgan, as Philip Young argues, is the direct outcome of the Spanish Civil War. As Young maintains, when Hemingway returned to America after his first visit to Spain, "he was ardently pro-Loyalist, he destroyed a good deal of the novel and changed the ending" (72-73).

Malcolm Cowley, as Allen Josephs (1989) quotes, believed that Harry Morgan's statement in *THAHN* was inserted by Hemingway after his visit to Spain (176).

Carlos Baker too corroborates Young's stand when he writes:

> It was clear that he wanted the book to document in some fashion his reconversion to social consciousness (*A Life Story*, 314).

In 1937, when Hemingway came to Spain as a *NANA* War Correspondent, his dispatches clearly showed his steady and rapid transformation. Coming in touch with the International militia and with the Spanish civilians and workers who ungrudgingly came forward to face death and to sacrifice anything that the cause needed, Hemingway was further impressed by the enthusiasm, courage, selflessness and, above all, a unique fellow-feeling and solidarity in the Spanish Civil War on the Republican side. This experience of the great "Spanish Tragedy" seems to have purged him of his feelings of self-centeredness, individuality, isolationism, and narrow parochialism. The very abstractions that he despised in *AFTA* became a reality in the Spanish Civil War.

Spain was not new to Hemingway. He knew Spain quite intimately, loved and appreciated its ancient sport of bullfight and identified himself with it. But the real or essential Spain was yet to be unfolded to him. That Hemingway realized in the course of his Spanish Civil War experience. The extent to which Hemingway was influenced by the Spanish Civil War could be guessed from the speech he delivered to the American writers and poets in the Carnegie hall:

> When men fight for the freedom of their country against a foreign invasion . . . and you know they were attacked and how they fought, at first almost unarmed, *You learn watching them live and fight and die, that there are worse things than wars. Cowardice is worse, treachery is worse, and simple selfishness is worse* (emphasis mine).

The above excerpt of the speech clearly explains Hemingway's transformation and the cause thereof. As Watkins observes, by the spring of 1938 Hemingway had abandoned his previous stand of 'separate peace' and of isolationism and was already writing in terms of "universal democratic idealism characteristic of *For Whom the Bell Tolls*" (140).

As we have already discussed, all the early protagonists were busy healing their own wounds inflicted by the irrational forces of this hostile world. They could hardly look beyond their own problems and misfortunes. Hence they were found introverted, withdrawing, thwarted individuals ever in their flight from one situation to another in a desperate bid to escape but are invariably caught and persecuted.

It is Harry Morgan, the last of the line, who, in his dying statement, utters the first cry of realization that dawned on the Hemingway protagonist largely out of the smoke and fire of the Spanish Civil War.

In the life of Robert Jordan and Anselmo the change is clear as it is in Philip Rawlings of *The Fifth Column* and some of the Spanish Civil War short stories.

Jordan believes in life, liberty and the pursuit of happiness. For him life is not as microscopic or atomic as that of his predecessors. The life that he leads is much larger, broader and more expansive than that of any of his predecessors. The very thought of the fall of the Republican in Spain is like a nightmare to him. As he says:

> If it were destroyed life would be unbearable for all
> those who believed in it (*FWBT*, 98).

Hemingway thus, as Allen Josephs rightly comments, "returns to become involved in mankind" (177) in the true spirit of Donnes' meditation. In sharp contrast to the negative, sentimental, nihilistic approach to life, as adopted by the line of protagonists from Nick Adams to Frederic Henry, Jordan shows a greatly positive response to life. He considers the world as a good place, "worth fighting for"(487). Jordan, unlike all his predecessors, has a strong reason and conviction:

> I have fought for what I believed in for a year now.
> If we win here we will win everywhere (*FWBT*, 46).

This conviction that Robert Jordan displays was grossly lacking in all the protagonists of Hemingway's pre-Spanish Civil War fictions. Jordan's conviction and his great commitment to a larger good is reflected in the following words. Jordan ruminates thus:

> You have to put many things in abeyance to win a war. If this war is lost all of those things are lost (*FWBT*, 305).

The above piece of Jordan's interior monologue shows his commitment to the cause and concern for his fellow-human beings which was not there in any of his predecessors.

Jordan (unlike Nick Adams or Frederic Henry) does not want to run away to a better and a safer place or to negotiate a "separate peace". He has no more the self-centeredness of his predecessors and his life is broad, liberated and highly altruistic compared to that of all his predecessors.

Jordan, in every bit of his action, tries his best to further the cause of mankind at large. Before he dies, he reflects:

> The world is a fine place and worth fighting for and I hate very much to leave it (*FWBT*, 487).

It may be noted that no other protagonist had found the world benign and lovable as Jordan did. That shows his positive attitude to life and his realization of the inherent truth in it.

The ensuing chapter will demonstrate in greater detail Hemingway's literary response to the Spanish Civil War and the corresponding change which his mode of writing underwent under the massive influence of his Spanish Civil War experience.

WORKS CITED

Allen, Josephs. *In Rewriting the Good Fight*, eds. Frieda S. Brown, et al. East Lansing, Michigan: Michigan University Press, 1989. 175-84.

Asselineau, Roger. *The Transcendentalist Constant in American Literature*. New York: New York University Press, 1980.

Baker, Carlos, ed. *Hemingway: Critiques of Four Major Novels*. New York: Scribners, 1962.

Baker, Carlos. *Hemingway: A Life Story*. Penguin, 1969.

Baker, Carlos. *Hemingway: The Writer as Artist*. Princeton, New Jersey: Princeton University Press, 1952.

Baker, Carlos, ed. *Ernest Hemingway: Selected Letters*, 1917-1961. New York: Scribners, 1981.

Baker, Sheridan . *Ernest Hemingway*. New York: Holt, Rinehart. 1967.

Benson, Jackson J. *Hemingway: The Writer's Art of Self-Defense*. Minneapolis: University of Minnesota Press, 1969.

Bloom, Harold, ed. *Ernest Hemingway's A Farewell to Arms*. New York: Chelsea House Publications, 1987.

Broer, Laurence R. *Hemingway's Spanish Tragedy*. Alabama: The University of Alabama Press, 1973.

Brooks Cleanth and R. Penn Warren. "The Killers" in *The Short Stories of Ernest Hemingway: Critical Essays*, ed. Jackson J. Benson. Durham, North Carolina: Duke University Press, 1975. 187-196.

Burhans, Clinton S. Jr. "The Complex of *In Our Time.*" *Modern Fiction Studies* 14-3 (Autumn 1968): 313-28.

Cowley, Malcolm. "Nightmare and Rituals in Hemingway." In *Hemingway: A Collection of Critical Essays*, ed. Robert P. Weeks, Englewood Cliffs, N. J.: Prentice-Hall , 1962, 40-51.

Dahiya, Bhim S. *The Hero in Hemingway: Study in Development*. N. Delhi: Bahri Pub., 1978.

Das Gupta, Hemendralal. *Hemingway: An Expatriate in Search of Life in Europe*. Kharagpur, 1974.

De Falco, Joseph. *The Hero in Hemingway's Short Stories*. Pittsburgh: University of Pittsburgh Press, 1963.

Farrel, James T. "*The Sun Also Rises*" In *Ernest Hemingway: Critiques of Four Major Novels*, ed. Carlos Baker. New York: Scribners, 1962. 4-6.

Flora, Joseph M. *Hemingway's Nick Adams*. Baton Rouge and London: Louisiana State University Press, 1982.

Hemingway, Ernest, ed. *Men at War*. New York: Crown Publications, 1942.

Hemingway, Ernest. *The Snows of Killimanjaro and Other Stories*. Penguin, 1963.

Hicks, Granville. *The Great Tradition*. Macmillan, 1933.

Johnson, Edgar. "Farewell the Separate Peace (1940)" in *Ernest Hemingway: The Man and His Work*, ed. John K. M. Mc Caffery. Cleveland and New York: World Pub. Company, 1950. 130-142.

Johnson, Kenneth G. "The Great Awakening: Nick Adams and the Silkworms in 'Now I Lay Me'." *Hemingway Notes* 1-2 (Fall 1971): 7-10.

Nageswar Rao , E. *Ernest Hemingway: A Study of his Rhetoric*. New Delhi: A Heinemann, 1983.

Nahal, Chaman. *The Narrative Pattern in Ernest Hemingway's Fiction*. Rutherford. N. Jersey: F.D.UP, 1971.

Oldsey, Bernard. "Hemingway's Old Men": *Modern Fiction Studies* 1-3 (August 1955): 31-35.

Nakajima, Kenji. "Hemingway's View of Alienation in Soldier's Home." *Kyushu American Literature* 20 (June 1979): 21-27.

Plimpton, George. "An Interview with Ernest Hemingway". In *Hemingway and His Critics*, ed. Carlos Baker. New York: Hill and Wang, 1961. 19-37.

Rama Rao, P.G. *The Narrative Technique of Ernest Hemingway*. N Delhi: S. Chand, 1980.

Rovit, Earl. *Ernest Hemingway*. New Haven, Conn: College and Univ. Press, 1963.

Shakespeare, Willam. *King Lear* IV. 1:36-37. Arden Shakespeare, ed. Kenneth Muir. London: Methuen,1901.

Spilka, Mark. "The Death of Love in *The Sun Also Rises*". In *Hemingway and His Critics*, ed. Carlos Baker. New York: Hill and Wang, 1961. 80-92.

Steinke, James. Hemingway's 'In Another Country' and 'Now I Lay Me'. *Hemingway Review* 5-1 (Fall 1985): 32-39.

Stephens, Robert O. *Hemingway's Non-Fiction: The Public Voice*. Chapel Hill: University of North Carolina Press, 1968.

Waldhorn, Arthur. *A Reader's Guide to Ernest Hemingway*. New York: Farrar, Straus and Giroux, 1972.

Watkins, Floyd C. *The Flesh and the World.* Nasheville: Vanderbilt University Press, 1971.

West, Ray B. Jr. "*A Farewell to Arms*" in *Ernest Hemingway: Critiques of Four Major Novels*, ed. Carlos Baker. New York: Scribners, 1962.

White, William, ed. *By-Line: Ernest Hemingway*. New York: Scribners, 1967.

Young, Philip. *Ernest Hemingway*. New York: Rinehart, 1952.

Young, Philip. *Ernest Hemingway: A Reconsideration*. University Park: Pennsylvania State University Press, 1966.

Young, Philip. "*The Sun Also Rises*: A Commentary." *Ernest Hemingway: Critiques of Four Major Novels*, ed. Carlos Baker, New York: Scribners, 1962. 7-10.

CHAPTER II

"NO MAN IS AN ILAND"

Hemingway was not even twenty when he joined the First World War as a member of the Redcross Ambulance crew, and got severely wounded. This experience sustained the young writer a pretty long period through his fictional writings. The trauma of the wounding affected Hemingway much more than the thrill of the war that possibly had prompted him to get enlisted. Obviously, almost all his fictional writings since the 1920s (When he started writing) show a consumming interest in violence.

The preceding chapter demonstrates how the horror of war has consistently found itself the central theme of all the short story collections and the two novels (*The Sun Also Rises* and *A Farewell to Arms*) of the 20s. But it is quite surprising to find that except in a few stories there is no direct reference to war anywhere. We have already discussed stories like "Now I Lay Me", "A Way You'll Never Be", "In Another Country" and some Vignettes of *In Our Time* where the wounded protagonist refers to the nightmare of war. In most of the stories, on the other hand, the after-effects of the war on its victims like Nick Adams are shown at length. The famous story "The Big-Two-Hearted River" is typical of this approach of the writer to the war. Years later, describing the composition of this story, Hemingway wrote in *A Moveable Feast*:

> The story was about coming back from the war but there was no mention of the war in it (76).

Finally, Hemingway's accumulated experience, reaction and inspiration got culminated in *A Farewell to Arms*. The approach to life and reality as we see in Frederic Henry has already been discussed in the previous chapter. In the course of the novel, Frederic Henry is repeatedly asked why he joined the war. And invariably, everytime, Henry either tries to avoid the issue or gives an evasive reply. Early in the book, on one occasion when Catherine Barkley asks Frederic, he says:

> I don't know. There is not always an explanation for everything (*AFTA*, 18).

Again, later, when a bartender asks him why he went to war, Frederic says:

> "I don't know. I was a fool" (*AFTA*, 256).

In "Now I Lay Me" the orderly John asks Nick why he joined the war. The answer that Nick gives him is quite similar to Frederic Henry's:

Nick Says:

"I don't know, John I wanted to, then" (*NAS*, 150). Stephen Cooper says:

> Whatever romantic or idealistic notions of the war Frederic Henry may have had are quickly destroyed by the reality of the war (37).

Further, when Frederic leaves the line, escapes through the river and joins Catherine in the Hotel, he even hates to read the newspaper, to hear anything about the war.

It becomes evident that no conviction, no commitment, no strong reason ever prompted Henry to go to war. It was a youthful euphoria, a sense of adventure and a vague ideal that prompted him to go to war (which Malcolm Cowley aptly calls "spectatorial"). And that precisely explains why Frederic Henry got disillusioned and dejected about the whole thing so soon.

Whereas, the cases of Robert Jordan, and even Philip Rawlings (*The Fifth Column*), are very different. They are almost of Henry's age and are in love like Henry and pressurized directly or indirectly to look forward to some cozy place of comfort and privacy, away from the war-torn Spain. It was directly in the case of Philip Rawlings, as the lady wants him to go for a 'separate peace', like Frederic Henry, and indirectly in the case of Jordan, because his girl Maria has been more sinned against than sinning. After a long spell of trauma and despair, since she was violated by the Fascists and found her parents killed, it was Jordan who gave her the first ray of hope. Thus, for Jordan, there is enough moral responsibility to ensure her happiness.

But no pressure, no temptation, no sentiment succeeds in breaking their commitment. They remain firm simply because of their commitment to the cause, their awareness of the individual's inherent and inalienable bond with the larger mankind beyond one's self. This awareness, this realization, in turn, brings these protagonists to their final target, the thing they had been seeking right from the beginning from young Nick Adams through Jake Barnes and Frederic Henry. What a deep commitment and a complete identification this piece of monologue shows as Jordan ruminates!

> I have fought for what I believed in for a year now.
> If we win here we will win everywhere (*FWBT*, 467).

This awareness of the human solidarity, a feeling of universal brotherhood, is the clear, visible part of the transformation that Hemingway's protagonist underwent after the Spanish Civil War.

In Hemingway's writing career two political events of his life had a significant decisive influence. One was the First World War; the other, the Spanish Civil War. In both the cases he did not fight directly but participated actively. While in the First World War he was seriously wounded, he passed through the Spanish Civil War safe and intact. But both the experiences had far-reaching impact on his writing, though in different directions.

The early writings of Hemingway, as we have already discussed, were entirely the writer's post-war creations, and carried unmistakably the deep mark of his exposure to the horror of war. The works, therefore, present a negative, rather nihilistic approach to life in general. And their protagonists, whom Philip Young rightly calls the "generic Nick Adams", or Carlos Baker calls "The Wastelanders", invariably suffer from an acute sense of insecurity, ineffectuality and disillusionment.

Whereas, Hemingway's participation in the Spanish Civil War brought about a drastic change in his approach to life in general, from the hitherto negative and nihilistic approach to a highly positive and constructive one. The feeling of insecurity, ineffectuality, sentimentality, purposelessness and narrow individualism gave way to confidence, vigor, boldness, conviction, affiliation and commitment to mankind at large.

Besides, the Spanish Civil War inspired Hemingway to write extensively on his experience that finally brought about one great novel, *For Whom the Bell Tolls*, one play, *The Fifth Column*, one film script, *The Spanish Earth*, six short stories and thirty war dispatches of great distinction.

In these writings, fact and fiction freely interplay as the barrier between the two is fragile and blurred. An examination of Hemingway's war dispatches will show how some of them were later reconstructed into stories and, how at many points, the dispatches anticipate the novel, *For Whom the Bell Tolls*, which was to come out almost two years later.

Hemingway had gone to Spain with a contract from *NANA* (North American Newspaper Alliance) to report on the Spanish Civil War. He sent thirty-one dispatches from there out of which twenty-eight were printed in different newspapers throughout the United States, Canada, and various countries in Europe at that time. In *By-Line: Ernest Hemingway* (1967) William White reprinted nine of them, and the rest of the dispatches were in obscurity till *The Hemingway Review* brought out all the existing thirty dispatches in an anthology for the first time, in its spring issue of 1988. The first dispatch was written on March 12, 1937 and the last on May 10, 1938. The period of his reporting was a little more than a year and covered the most crucial phase of the Spanish Civil War. Hemingway, in the course of his reporting, shows his deep political insight, historic sense, and his knowledge of geography and military strategy. The dispatches bear ample evidence of the fact that right from the time of his arrival in Spain Hemingway realized the genuineness of the Republican cause till the very end. But it should not be construed that his dispatches were pro-Republican and anti-Fascist only. His dispatches conveyed the situation of war from time to time in an honest and truthful manner with the obvious limitations of a reporter operating in a chaotic situation in which a ruthless press censorship distorted the facts beyond recognition.

As the editors of this anthology of dispatches in the special issue of the *Hemingway Review* painfully observe:

> What he wrote and what newspaper readers in America and elsewhere read were not the same things. Days of hard work, days of personal risk, days of intense cold or heat, some days with little sleep at the end of them—all this to get a story out that would then be caught or suppressed or altered in ways the correspondent couldn't control.... The printed story, therefore, was often a truncated, adulterated version of what had been written (*HR*. 7-2. Spring 1988:3).

Hemingway, despite all such handicaps, continued to remain faithful to his job till the very end. As I have pointed out at the beginning of this chapter, the Spanish Civil War was to play a significant and decisive role in the life of Hemingway as a writer. As soon as he arrived in Spain as a *NANA* correspondent, he was instantly drawn to the cause of the democratic republic that was gravely in danger under the threat of Fascism. This sudden change in Hemingway's attitude to life and society is clearly felt when one compares his response, in the context of America's involvement in any European crisis, a few months before, with its sudden reversal soon after he arrived on the Spanish front. We have already discussed this point at length in the previous chapter.

It is quite interesting to note that long before the Western powers realized that the Spanish Civil War could be a potential threat to their safety and integrity, Hemingway (and Orwell too) had first sounded the alarm call and pronounced prophetically its dangerous consequences. In all his journalistic jottings of this period, such as the *NANA* dispatches, articles for *Ken, Pravda*, his script for the film *The Spanish Earth*, and his address to the second American Writers' Congress in Carnegie Hall, Hemingway consistently and unequivocally pointed out the dangerous possibilities of the Spanish Civil War if the Republicans failed in their resistance. He has raised a continuous alarm and urged all the Western countries to realize that Spain gave them the last and the ultimate chance to save Democracy. As he asserted in Carnegie Hall:

> There is only one form of Government that cannot produce good writers, and that system is Fascism (Baker, *Life*, 478).

That partly explains why Hemingway was so much drawn to the internal conflict of Spain, a minor European country and a peripheral power. The other factors responsible for bringing about such dramatic transformation of Hemingway will be clear in the process of examining the war dispatches, the short stories, the film script, the play, and the novel that Hemingway wrote on the Spanish Civil War theme.

II

The thirty *NANA* dispatches that Hemingway wrote during the most critical phase of the Spanish Civil War give the harrowing picture of untold atrocities and violence perpetrated by the Fascists on the civilian population of Spain. They show the chaotic atmosphere of Spain, in general, and Madrid, in particular, with frequent shellings and strafings by the Fascist air force. Amidst all the details of this wild violence, Hemingway's profound humanitarianism is reflected in his concern for his fellow human beings, irrespective of racial and national barriers. The uncertainty, horror and misery of the people during the war is portrayed in vivid detail. At times, the situation is dramatized in a highly artistic manner, keeping the tragic undertone of the issue intact.

By and large, the dispatches, with their maddening variety and diversity, project inevitably the writer's genuine concern for human suffering. This very aspect is a clear manifestation of his change of attitude to life, and Carlos Baker rightly calls it Hemingway's "recent conversion to social consciousness" (*Life*, 478). It shows a marked improvement upon his protagonists' general egocentric approach to life as found in *The Sun Also Rises* and *A Farewell to*

Arms. Now onwards the protagonists demonstrate a remarkably affirmative approach to life. They see things not through the narrow perspective of their own individual self, but through a broader, larger perspective of common social considerations and values.

In a few dispatches we notice Hemingway reporting the matter in a comical and lighter vein, making the whole atmosphere genial and lively. They look like comic interludes in a tragedy.

Another important aspect of the dispatches worth noting is that out of the on-the-spot reporting on war-torn Spain, Hemingway found and later incorporated several plots into some of his short stories. Even, there is a general consensus of critical opinion that the very portrayal of the protagonist of Hemingway's Spanish Civil War novel, *For Whom the Bell Tolls*, is based on a real life figure who participated in the Civil War, and that Hemingway makes a special mention of his gallantry in the war.

Thus it becomes imperative to examine the text of some of the key dispatches to explore the nature of Hemingway's transformation and to reaffirm the corresponding changes that followed in his writing. Carlos Baker has this to say on Hemingway's intention behind his acceptance of *NANA* reportership:

> His intent in working for the *NANA* would be to serve as anti-war war correspondent seeking to keep the United States from becoming involved in the future conflict (*Life*, 456).

But interestingly, as we find from the very first dispatch, Hemingway, who just a short while ago was a great advocate of American isolationism (from any sort of European or international crisis), gets miraculously transformed as soon as he lands in Spain. In this (first) dispatch which he files from Toulouse, dated March 12, 1937, Hemingway strongly resents the U.S. Non-intervention policy. He points out that, while the United States is observing its "strictest neutrality", Italy is busy pumping its forces and weaponry into the hands of the insurgents to be used against the Republicans and the Civilians (*HR*, Spring 1988:14).

Such is the change, the transformation that swept Hemingway thoroughly as a man and an artist as well. It reminds one of Orwell's transformation at the magic touch of the Spanish Civil War atmosphere we have discussed in the first chapter.

We may recall how Hemingway went back to the U.S.A. after his first visit and madly pursued his mission of fund-raising and arousing public opinion in favour of the Spanish Republic. With his shyness, he gave his first public (and formal) speech to the Second American Writers' Conference in Carnegie Hall and willingly accepted several offices of responsibility to aid the Spanish Republic. All this dedicated and enthusiastic endeavour that Hemingway voluntarily undertook is amply suggestive of his warmth, sincerity and commitment to the cause.

The ghastly, diabolical aspects of the horror of war catch Hemingway's attention most. He is horrified seeing the indiscriminate bombing of the civilian population. As he reports in his dispatch dated April 11, 1937:

> They killed an old woman returning home from the market, dropping her in a huddled black heap of clothing, with one leg suddenly detached whirling against the wall of an adjoining house (27).

Invariably, like the old woman here the innocent civilians were the inevitable victims of the carnage. In the next dispatch, Hemingway reports how after an aerial attack he sees a policeman covering "the top of the trunk from which the head is missing" (30).

More shocking than such ghastly murder is the growing apathy of the people. As Hemingway writes in his usual understatement:

> "The dead man was not you nor any one you know and everyone is very hungry up at the Guadalajara front" (30).

In another dispatch, dated March 22, 1937 from Madrid, Hemingway gives yet another account of such senseless, brutal killing. This time he reports on the death of some Italian soldier fighting for the insurgents. He painfully describes how these three Italians are lying dead "with waxy gray faces":

> They did not look like men, but... like curiously *broken toys* (19) (emphasis mine).

In the description of such gruesome violence, Hemingway's profound humanitarianism emerges clear. This account of the Italian's killing partly speaks against the unjust allegation that Hemingway's reporting was pro-Loyalist and anti-Fascist. Secondly, the above account makes one aware of the fragility and transience of human life—a rare phenomenon in the quasi-existential Hemingway world.

On another occasion, Hemingway's broad humanitarianism is reflected in his response to a dead rebel officer:

> "We ...left him with his serious waxen face where tanks could not bother him now or anything else" (87).

This shows how Hemingway responded to the suffering and death of a friend and a foe as well. This is another evidence of his broad humanism.

Another significant angle of Hemingway's art of reporting is his sense of detachment (which Orwell admits to have cultivated since *Homage to Catalonia* (*CEJL*: I, 29). A poet as he was basically, in his taste and sensibility, Hemingway is often seen relapsing into his poetic self in the midst of bombing and strafing. While coming into Valencia through the dark highway he could feel the sweet smell of the orange grooves in full bloom and he writes that it seemed "to this half-asleep correspondent like a wedding" (18).

In another dispatch there is a wonderful mixture of the serious and the comic which only a deeply detached artist like Hemingway could accomplish. In this dispatch, dated April 14,1938, Hemingway reports on the suspected routing of the Lincoln Washington battalion including the great Robert Merriman (who later served as Hemingway's model for Robert Jordan in *FWBT*) in a somewhat comic manner. He describes the overturned truck with its load of ripe oranges on its way to the front:

> But nobody touched his oranges and they lay a shining yellow tribute to something as we pulled out of there (72).

In his 24th dispatch, dated April 15, 1938, Hemingway shows another feat of artistic detachment while serving a heavily disheartening news on the Republican defeat with dispassion and complete self-control. In fact, this was a major and decisive breakthrough of the Fascist forces across the painfully guarded defences of the Republican militias over months. As Hemingway gives an effective visual aid:

> Ahead of us all this time the Heinkels were circling and diving with the mechanical monotony of the movement of a quiet afternoon at a six-day bike race (80-81).

Again, he reports on the enthusiastic action of the young Republican volunteers in the face of defeat and despair:

> Boys were working, hammering and nailing and sawing as fast and hard as a good crew on a vessel in distress at sea (82).

The image is so befitting and the spirit so natural in this recreation of the atmosphere that despite the gravity of the situation the reporter's art and imagination come out conspicuously. In this dispatch the picture of evacuation of the civilians from the Ebro basin anticipates Hemingway's famous short story, "Old Man at the Bridge".

Another lively piece of reportage that we come across is the one which Hemingway sent from Paris on his way back after his first trip. This finally came out subsequently as a short-story with the title "The Chauffeurs of Madrid". In this dispatch Hemingway gives an account of his four successive drivers in his tours across the country. In the process, Hemingway draws the character in such imaginative yet vivid detail that they almost represent a cross-section of Spanish people with their typical as well as common features. Those four chauffeurs largely represented the Spanish Republic, with all their virtues and vices, their strengths and weaknesses. As this dispatch was later on developed into a story it would be better to take it up along with Hemingway's other stories on the Spanish Civil War.

When one goes through these war dispatches from Spain, another thing that impresses us is Hemingway's sense of history, geography, and even a fair measure of military tactics and strategy.

For example, in a comparatively lengthy dispatch, dated May 9,1937, Hemingway makes a very insightful analysis of the fate of the Spanish Civil War in the perspective of the American Civil War and the Russian Revolution. As he reflects, during the four-year struggle, the federal troops in America were thoroughly forged and stood like a granite wall on which Gen. Lee's Army "rose and curled and fell". In Russia too, despite a series of debacles, the Red Army triumphed finally because of "a united people, geography and time"(40). On the basis of these evidences of history, Hemingway's analysis ends in an optimistic note in favor of a Republican victory in Spain.

In this dispatch, Hemingway's sound historic sense and wonderful power of assimilation is reflected. Besides, in an attempt at analyzing the battles of Brihuega and of Bilbao, Hemingway shows a keen sense of geography and a knowledge of the logistics of warfare when he concludes like any professional military strategist that Madrid is simply an "impregnable fortress" (40).

Another situation that Hemingway reports in his dispatch dated October 6,1937 from Madrid shows his insightful analysis and his diplomatic perception of the issue. Speaking of the rebel strong-holds he reports:

> They are holding fortified towns unconnected by any defenses, but which dominate the country around them as castles did in the feudal days (58).

Again , Hemingway's keen diplomatic perception enables him to see the skull beneath the skin. As he writes:

> The fate of Spain is being decided in Berlin, where Mussolini and Hitler are conferring (59).

Very much like a war-expert, Hemingway sends his analysis of the latest strategic position adopted by both the armies. As he writes about Franco's:

> Franco's tactics in this whole offensive have been to feel for the soft points and, finding them, concentrate artillery and planes to make the break ... (78).

It is well acknowledged that in Hemingway's writings fact and fiction overlap frequently and with felicity. As we have seen in the case of "The Chauffeurs of Madrid" many such facts were later converted into fiction directly or obliquely. For instance, in one of the early dispatches Hemingway says:

> This is a strange new kind of war where you learn just as much as you are able to believe (33).

This very observation of Hemingway gets into his novel, *For Whom the Bell Tolls*, in the course of time (where the protagonist makes an identical statement).

In another dispatch, dated September 3, 1937, from Valencia, Hemingway makes a special mention of the great heroic performance of an American University professor who subsequently served as the model for Robert Jordan in *For Whom the Bell Tolls* (1940). As Hemingway reports:

> Robert Merriman, a former California professor and now chief of staff of the 15th brigade was a leader in the final assault. Unshaven, his face smoke blackened, his men tell how he bombed his way forward, wounded six times . . . but refusing to have his wounds dressed until the cathedral was taken (49).

Similarly, one of the most popular and oft-cited Spanish Civil War stories of Hemingway, "Old Man at the Bridge", is based upon his dispatch that he sent from Tortosa dated April 15, 1938. The dispatch draws a vivid picture of the evacuation of civilian population in the wake of the collapse of Republican resistance. As Hemingway reports, "It was a four-fingered push towards the sea"(81). And about the bombing that went on unabated Hemingway writes:

> Above us in the high cloudless sky fleet after fleet of bombers roared over Tortosa. When they dropped the sudden thunder of their loads, the little city on the Ebro disappeared in a yellow mounting cloud of dust. The dust never settled as more bombers came and finally it hung like a yellow fog all down the Ebro valley (80).

Thus, in the course of Hemingway's war dispatches from Spain the many-sided talent of Hemingway is revealed. His accuracy of reporting, his objectivity, his thorough grasp of the matter, and his insightful analysis are evident besides his sound sense of history and geography. Above all, his artistic detachment and craftsmanship leave strong impressions on the Reader's mind. Even when describing the most crucial situations, Hemingway shows his great restraint by not allowing his emotion to run high and presenting the stark reality with dispassion.

Another important point worth noting is the emergence of Hemingway's "hitherto well-hidden social consciousness" (*Life*, 487), a remarkable transformation that is reflected clearly in the dispatches.

The vivid presentation of the gruesome violence that Hemingway saw with his own eyes, to my thinking, served as an effective antidote to counteract the trauma he carried since his wounding at Fossalta in the First World War. As Carlos Baker observed in this context:

> His first visit to war time Spain had destroyed his belief in the after-life, but it had also eliminated all his fear of death . . . (*Life*, 481).

In dealing with the Spanish Civil War dispatches it would not be possible to deal with Hemingway's other writings during the period strictly according to chronology. As such, Hemingway visited Spain four times during the course of the troubled Civil War period and spent about a year in Madrid on several fronts. His dispatches naturally covered the entire span from the point he arrived in Spain for reporting till he finally left broken-hearted seeing the imminence of the fall of the Republic.

It was during the first visit (March 1932-May 1937) itself that Hemingway plunged headlong into the production of a documentary film entitled *The Spanish Earth*, and during his second visit (August 1937-August 1938) he made a sincere attempt to write a realistic play, *The Fifth Column*, from a Madrid Hotel when the city was under heavy fire. Besides, many of his short stories were written in the course of his four visits to Spain during the Civil War period.

The very idea of the film and the project was initiated by a group of pro-Loyalist American intellectuals called "Contemporary Historians". Besides Hemingway, the group comprised novelist John Dos Passos, play-wright Lillian Hellman and poet Archibald Macleish. But eventually the whole thing was managed by Hemingway with the Dutch director Jorish Ivens and the photographer John Ferno. The shots were taken in actual war conditions often under direct fire and aerial bombing.

Besides helping the shooting all along, Hemingway gave the script and the voice for its commentary. The emotionally charged voice and the words straight from his heart made the film deeply evocative and served its purpose immensely. The film was intended to serve two objectives. First, it was supposed to counter the pro-Fascist press campaign that catered blatant lies and distorted facts in America and the world around. Second, it was to be shown for raising funds to equip the medical and ambulance corps for the Republican army. And precisely, the film did its job excellently well.

The film, in fact, is a series of random shots in six-reel showing the real Spanish tragedy as projected on the terrible plight of the Spanish people. Particular care is taken to focus the camera eye on the agonized women, old men, children, gypsies and the young recruits and soldiers. Arthur Coleman rightly comments that "it is more precisely a general report of suffering than a political commentary" very much in the manner of "Picasso's *Guernica* (*HR*, Fall 1982: 64). The film concentrates on two aspects of the Spanish life: The inherent bond between the peasants and their land, the dislocation, chaos and tragedy that the internecine conflict has brought about. "It is a picture which tells the truth and not a pack of dirty lies", thus says Jasper Wood in his introduction to the script (ii). The film opens with Hemingway's words in his own voice:

> The Spanish Earth is dry and hard and the faces of
> the men who work on that earth are hard and dry
> from the sun (*The Spanish Earth*, 19).

The simple, primitive Spanish peasants, who are ever contented with their little necessaries like potato, wine and onion have been long denied their rightful share of land and harvest. Now they make a fresh renewed attempt to reclaim their land, to irrigate them and to reap their harvest.

The camera then quickly moves to shoot the "true face of men going to action". The houses are left empty except for the few survivors of the aerial bombardment who are in the trenches now. As the editor comments: "this picture wasn't acted, it is what is real and true and horrible" (12). The commentary too mentions the same: "Men cannot act before the camera in the presence of death" (23).

The commentary arouses profound pathos as when Julian, a young recruit on the front, writes a letter to his father in the village:

> Papa, I will be there in three days. Tell our mother (24).

The audience is left to speculate whether the boy could really keep his promise in the horrible uncertainty of the time. But the tension is dramatically released when Julian catches an empty truck and reaches home "sooner than he expected"(42). Then the Camera moves and the commentary comes:

> You stand in line all day to buy food for supper, sometimes the foods run out before you reach the door. Sometimes a shell falls near the line and at home they wait and wait and no body brings back anything for supper (41).

The camera then focuses on a book-keeper on his way to his office in the morning "who has nothing to do with War" absolutely. The commentary follows:

> So now they take the book-keeper away, but not to his office or to his home (41).

Such typical understatement of Hemingway in the commentary, like his stories and novels, adds a special appeal.

Moving to the front has become a regular feature now. The typical scene of a married man going to battle is frequent, pathetic and moving. The commentary runs:

> They say the good-byes that sound the same in any language. She says she'll wait. He says that he'll come back. . . . No body knows if he'll come back.

> Take care of the kid, he says. . . . They both know that when they move you out in trucks, it's to a battle (45).

Then the commentary reminds us of how "Death comes each morning" (45) to the people of this town from the rebels in the hills. And there is a strong appeal to the olfactory sense when the commentary asserts:

> The smell of death is acrid high explosive smoke and blasted granite (45).

Hemingway does not preserve his feelings for the Spaniards alone. His concern for the dead Italians who fought for the Fascists is equally deep and genuine.

This film, though a minor project compared to Hemingway's other more impressive literary response to the Civil War in Spain, is a great trend-setter. During the course of his involvement in the production and the subsequent presentation of the documentary Hemingway shows his great commitment and devotion to the cause. After the shooting was done in a situation where life was at risk every moment, the commentary was written, as Jasper Wood writes, "in bomb-ridden hotels and in the seclusion of continually shelled trenches" (12). That was not all. When the film was ready, Hemingway, with his image and influence, saw to it that the premiere was arranged at the White House, and they were the honoured guests of President Roosevelt. Then he moved on to California to make a show for the film colony to raise funds for the ambulances and medical supplies for the Loyalists. F. Scott Fitzgerald, who was there at one such gathering, later recalled how Hemingway blew into Hollywood like a whirlwind and radiated an intensity that had "something almost religious about it", scooping up close to 14,000 dollars in a single evening. (*Fitzgerald Letters*, 300-1)

This shows the dramatic transformation of this great artist from an isolationist stand to a total identification with a purely humanistic cause. Besides, the commentary of the film, as the initial response of Hemingway to any common cause, looks forward to his subsequent major literary work, *For Whom the Bell Tolls*.

For instance, the focus on La Passionaria, the most famous woman of the Spanish Civil War in this film, anticipates his treatment of women in *For Whom the Bell Tolls*. "She is not a romantic beauty", the commentary clarifies. "She is", on the other hand, "the wife of a poor miner in Asturias". She is not an individual, for she represents the million voices of "the new Spanish Women". And the commentary stresses the point that "it is a new nation forged in the discipline of the bravery of its women" (32).

Hemingway's broad vision of common humanity, that runs through the entire novel, *For Whom the Bell Tolls*, is clearly anticipated in the brief commentary of this documentary. In the course of the commentary Hemingway mentions the sad letters found invariably from the dead Italian soldiers in Spain. This very fact closely anticipates the Fascist whom Jordan kills in the morning only to discover from the letter in his pocket that he came from a village that Jordan knew so well (*FWBT*, 302).

In spite of all its merits this piece of documentary, however, did not receive universal acclaim. A reviewer in the *New York Times* dismissed the film, particularly Hemingway's narrative, as mere propaganda (Manus, *New York Times,* August 37:7). A distinguished film critic, Ferguson, however, comments that the film's speciality lies in its "abstention from bombast and sloganism". He calls attention to the "Carrying power" that Hemingway's understatement gives it (*Philip*, 35).

III

After the successful production of the documentary, *The Spanish Earth*, Hemingway's second literary response to the Spanish Civil War was a full-length play, *The Fifth Column*. He wrote this play in a hotel when Madrid was under siege and its fall was imminent (October 1937). During the period of writing, as Hemingway mentions in his preface, the hotel "was struck by more than thirty high explosive shells (v). Hugh Thomas, in his famous book *The*

Spanish Civil War, corroborates Hemingway's note on the nightmarish atmosphere of the time (495).

Set very realistically in Madrid, mostly in the Hotel Florida, the piece is a three-act play on the theme of counterespionage, with the conflict of love and duty, of individual happiness and social commitment as its central motif. The main character, Philip Rawlings, is an American correspondent secretly engaged in counterespionage for the Loyalists. He lives in Hotel Florida and leads an apparently affluent and bohemian life. By the time the play begins and we see him, he says that he has been in the job for about a year. We see him somewhat tense and worn out possibly owing to the dangerous nature of his job. As he confesses to another official of the same Loyalist counterespionage ring, Antonio:

> With me it's on the nerves now for a long time....
> Too bloody much. And I am . . . tired too (44).

Obviously, the unsavory nature of his job got on his nerves and he feels as if he were in a veritable "death-trap" (85). May be for the exhaustion and weariness he, for quite some time, thinks of marriage, home, and a sort of quasi-separate peace . In the course of this phase of fatigue and exhaustion, Philip speaks out to Antonio that he "would like to marry a girl named Bridges" because "she's got the longest, smoothest, straightest legs in the world"(44).

Philip's conflict gets deepened and we hear him talking repeatedly about his run down state of mind. He again tells Antonio complaining:

> I am very tired, see, and I am also disgusted with my job, and I'm nervous as a bastard because I'm worried . . . (53).

The persisting tension of the circumstances in which he operates strains him very badly and he looks forward desperately to some possible means of release and relief. As he tells Dorothy, "I'd like to marry you, and go away, and get out of all this" (75).

Harriet Fellner observes on this crisis of Philip:

> In *The Fifth Column,* where Madrid's oppressive atmosphere is again linked to the shelling, the bombardment also serves as a back drop for the Venus-Mars conflict (74).

At this point of the play Philip seems to be a continuation of Nick Adams, Jake Barnes and Frederic Henry. He is weak, he is threatened and he wants to run away from reality. But this period of weakness and proposed escape of Philip, unlike in the case of all his predecessors, does not stay long. We soon find him gathering himself up wonderfully and asserting his commitment to the greater cause. Gone are those thoughts of marriage, home, privacy, quietness, personal comforts and happiness.

The brief conflict between his own self and mankind at large finally resolves. Philip stands fully to execute the death-bed conversion of Harry Morgan in *To Have and Have Not*. When Philip's friend Max asks him about his commitment to Dorothy, he replies resolutely and unequivocally:

> "I'm going to break it with her" (101).

He further declares:

> We're in for fifty years of undeclared wars and
> I've signed up for the duration (101).

Presently, Philip has no wavering, no indecision, no conflict. His revulsion for the dirty job of counterespionage, his sickness for war and violence, temporarily makes him disillusioned about the cause he is committed to. But the spell goes away as quickly as it comes. The conflict between personal comfort and happiness on the one hand, and social responsibility and commitment on the other, fails to obstruct the powerful urge for self-abnegation.

In his last meeting with Dorothy, Philip shows his decisiveness, clarity of vision, and his firmness when he dismisses her passionate appeal thus:

> And where I go now I go alone, or with others, who
> go there for the same reason I go (104).

This changing response, as it becomes clear in the above statement of Philip, is in sharp contrast to the attitude manifested in all his predecessors including Harry Morgan, save his moment of realization before his death.

At this point of our discussion it may be relevant to refer to the Carnegie Hall speech of Hemingway to the Second American

Writers' Congress. In the course of his seven-minute speech, amidst thunderous applause, Hemingway called upon his fellow writers to "write truly" and to project one's findings of truth "in such a way that it becomes part of the experience of the person who reads it" (Baker. *Life*, 477).

In his play, *The Fifth Column,* Hemingway has made a consistent attempt to project his experience in the most realistic manner without much artistic restraint. Carlos Baker points out the extensive autobiographical parallels:

> Rawlings had 'big shoulders and a walk like a gorilla', commonly skipped breakfast, read all morning papers . . . drank regularly at Chicote's Bar . . . (*Life*, 488).

The very setting of the play is mostly in the Hotel Florida of Madrid where Hemingway himself was staying, and the lady correspondent Dorothy Bridges resembles Martha Gellhorn, with her long smooth legs (488).

IV

Hemingway thus draws his emotions from his real experience in life and transmutes them into art, not of course in a Wordsworthian sense strictly (Tanner, 4). What Hemingway thought to be his points of strength by giving the factual details are treated as his points of failure by the critics. The critical consensus settles largely on his failure as a playwright. However, after the Theater Guild had adapted the play the situation improved and the play started receiving a favorable response. To Brooks Atkinson, it was a "strikingly convincing drama" (*New York Times*, March 7,1940:18), while Joseph Wood Krutch saw it as a "fine play" and felt greatly optimistic about its success (*Critical Heritage*, 291).

On the other hand, critics like Edgar Johnson and Edwin Berry Burgum believe that the Spanish Civil War experience was the main driving force behind the transformation of both Hemingway and his hero (Stephens, 217). Like Philip Young, Edgar Johnson too attributes the transition in Hemingway's writing to his first visit to Spain after the outbreak of the Civil War. This is reflected in the ending of *To Have and Have Not*. They further argue that after coming back from Spain after his first forty-five days' stay, Hemingway made some important change in the ending of *To Have and Have Not*. As Edgar Johnson clearly maintains, Harry Morgan's realization of the futility of his singular individual attempt to win a victory is a step forward to the "tone of social co-operation" in *The Fifth Column* (*Sewanee Review*, XLVIII 1940: 289-90). Similarly, Edwin Berry Burgum considered the Spanish Civil War as instrumental in his transformation from "Bohemianism to Democracy" (*New Masses* November 22,1938:21). John M. Muste, commenting on the clear transition from Hemingway's earlier writings (which we may call the pre-Spanish Civil War writings as well) to his later (Spanish Civil War and post-Spanish Civil War) writings, says:

> The play presents a stoic posturing in the face of danger and hardship which almost parodies such earlier Hemingway heroes as Jake Barnes and Frederic Henry (66).

Thus all the pre-Spanish Civil War protagonists of Hemingway including Harry Morgan (till the moment of his fatal injury that precedes his ultimate realization) are grossly immersed in their own selfish pursuits. The young Nick Adams is ever on his heels in frantic effort to save his skin. Jake Barnes is running hopelessly from Paris to Pamplona in search of peace and stability for his restless mind and self. Frederic Henry, in his escapade from the war front, is desperately attempting to make a separate peace for his own future and happiness. Harry Morgan too succumbs to the injury that he has received in his strife to bring comfort and cheer to his small family. But it is in Harry's last words that we see the transformation, with the shifting of emphasis from the narrow bounds of his self to the larger world beyond, taking shape. But Harry does not live to bring his life's realization to action. And it is Philip Rawlings (*The Fifth Column*) who fulfils the sacred ritual, the last wish of Harry, the desired object of the continual search of all the protagonists since Nick Adams.

As Angel Capellan asserts:

> The central and most decisive element in Hemingway's fiction is the presence of a protagonist whom we can follow from childhood to old age, through several reincarnations and adaptations (67).

In view of the seminal role that Philip Rawlings performs in the growth of Hemingway's protagonist, *The Fifth Column*, despite its imperfections, serves as an indispensable link between *To Have and Have Not* and *For Whom the Bell Tolls*.

V

Apart from the dispatches, the documentary, the play and of course the much acknowledged novel, Hemingway has written six short stories on the Spanish Civil War background. Excepting "The Old Man at the Bridge" all other stories remained in obscurity since their publication in late thirties in *Esquire* and *Cosmopolitan* till as late as 1969 when Charles Scribner's Sons brought out four of them with *The Fifth Column*. In 1971 an anthology published from Moscow included another two from this group including "The Old Man at the Bridge". It was in 1987 finally that an anthology entitled *Hemingway's Complete Short Stories* brought out all these stories.

While Hemingway's writings received abundant critical response, these pieces were mostly deprived of such scholarly attention. Though apparently there seems to be no reason why this happened, the causes for this can possibly be two. First, after the disappointing fall of the Loyalists Hemingway himself did not take any interest in further inclusion of these stories in any of his anthologies. Secondly, the sentimental and partly propagandistic nature of these pieces did not attract any scholarly attention, particularly after the publication of the major novel *For Whom the Bell Tolls*.

But in the context of this study these stories, despite all their limitations, still have a relevance. It is because, very much like the dispatches, the documentary, and the play, these stories were the direct products of Hemingway's Spanish Civil War experience, and they further looked forward to his major work *For Whom the Bell Tolls*. In fact all of them were written during a period when the Loyalists were mostly on the defensive and their line of control was fast receding. Besides, these stories reflect the various moods and aspects of the Civil War and show the transition that finally becomes conspicuous in *For Whom the Bell Tolls*. They cover varied themes ranging from conflict to resolution, futility to affirmation, senseless killing to spiritual transcendence and, above all, from self to selflessness.

The first of this series, "The Old Man at the Bridge", was published in *Ken* in its May 1938 issue.

In one of his late dispatches, we may recall, Hemingway mentions an old man whom he met near a pontoon bridge when there was a great exodus of civilians following the failure of a Republican resistance. In this story, in a thinly covered disguise, the narrator, a war correspondent obviously, relates his meeting with an old man.

Against the background of hectic movement, great tension, and apprehension, following the collapse of the Loyalist resistance, the narrator meets "an old man with steel rimmed spectacles and very dusty clothes sitting by the side of the road". Further up, the last batch of civilian refugees are hastily crossing the pontoon bridge. "But the old man sat there without moving. He was too tired to go any further."

> "Where do you come from?" asks the narrator.
> "From San Carlos," came the brief reply with a smile. "I was taking care of animals," the old man added.

He further tells that he was "the last one to leave the town of San Carlos" (Moscow ed., 311).

In the course of this brief conversation the narrator comes to know that the old man was greatly worried about his animals that he was forced to leave behind. As the old man says, "There were two goats, a cat and four pairs of pigeons" (312).

"And you have no family?" asks the narrator while his gaze was fixed on "the far end of the bridge where a few last carts were hurrying down the slope of the bank" (312).

"No," says the old man and adds that the animals that he mentioned are the only members of his family on earth. While talking with the narrator, the old man is busy analyzing the crisis to himself and feels slightly relieved to think about the cat who can look out for itself. Interrupting the old man in his deep concern for his animals the narrator asks again:

> "What politics have you?"
>
> "I am without politics," comes the reply (312).

But the old man ought to go somewhere, the narrator reminds him. "He looked at me very blankly and tiredly" (313), while the old man was lost in his thought for the animals. After feeling a little relieved about the cat, he remembers that the dove-cage has been unlocked which brings some more relief to his anxiety. Finally, not able to find any more clues for the possible escape of the goats, he instructs himself (in the manner of all later Hemingway protagonists at the hour of crisis and helplessness) not to think about them rather. "Then the old man tried to be on his feet, but he couldn't. He sat down backwards in the dust" (313).

> And the story ends at this point, with the narrator's note:
>
> There was nothing to do about him. It was Easter Sunday and the Fascists were advancing toward the Ebro. It was a gray overcast day with a low ceiling so their planes were not up. That and the fact that cats know how to look after themselves was all the good luck that old man would ever have (313).

This story, with its brevity, compactness and a profound tragic undertone, anticipates Hemingway's later works in more than one way. The great detachment, the negation of self and supreme commitment to his duty are strongly manifested in the character of the old man. Even at a moment, when his own life is under terrible threat, particularly in the chaotic, maddening atmosphere of evacuation in a war time situation, the sort of yogic detachment about his own self and safety that the old man shows is unparalleled. This supreme detachment, negation of the self and commitment to duty that make the character of the old man so admirable is a complete new trend that Hemingway's writings show in the wake of the Spanish Civil War. The old man thus looks forward to Robert Jordan and Santiago in Hemingway's two subsequent major works.

The next three stories that came out in *Esquire* between November 1938 and February 1939 are all set in Chicote's, a famous bar in Madrid. "The Denunciation," the first of this series, is based upon the conflict of self and social commitment. The story is set in Chicote's against a background of terrible tension when Madrid was under indiscriminate aerial bombing and heavy shelling.

The story is overtly autobiographical and thus shows the writer's initial apolitical stand. He makes it clear at the beginning as to why Chicote's was the best bar in Madrid. Besides its team of modest and decent attendants, Chicote's was one of the very few places where "you did not talk politics". With the break of the Civil War the regular visitors to this bar are now mostly on Franco's side while a few are committed to the Loyalists. Why the number of visitors committed to the Loyalist Camp has drastically fallen is reasoned out by the narrator thus:

> Because it was a very cheerful place, and because really cheerful people are usually the bravest, and the bravest get killed quickest, a big part of Chicote's old customer are now dead (*Complete S. Stories*, 421).

The above observation and analysis show the writer's existential awareness as it is reflected in Frederic Henry's perception of life in *A Farewell to Arms*. Soon we are introduced to the main crisis in the plot. The narrator confronts a grave moral crisis when one of the old waiters of Chicote's draws his attention to an old visitor and an old acquaintance of the narrator who is now a Fascist in the guise of a Loyalist sympathizer. The instant reaction of the narrator was isolationistic, noncommittal. "It's not my business," he sharply dismisses the waiter. The waiter who is an old man speaks out his own state of mind, his conflict between emotion and duty, by the way, mentions how he has a son on the front and another killed fighting for the peoples' cause. Nevertheless, the narrator continues to maintain his stand saying repeatedly, "It is thy problem, I am not a politician". But the old waiter wouldn't relent. He comes again finally with his conflict resolved by now and says, "It is my responsibility" (423). Under these circumstances the narrator feels pressurized and at last gives the telephone number of the secret police to the waiter and tries to wash his hands clean. While taking the telephone number the old waiter makes his stand clear to the narrator:

> "I have nothing against him. But it is the cause"(423).

Until this point the narrator, however, continues to maintain his stand. He does not want to denounce the man himself: "*But I am a foreigner and it is your war and your problem*" (emphasis mine). This very feeling of being a foreigner as a result of his failure to identify himself with the *causa* takes a drastic turn when the old waiter shows his high sense of duty and his commitment to the cause by denouncing the customer at last. Soon after passing on the information to the secret police over phone the waiter again comes and confesses:

> He was an old client and a good client. Also I have never denounced anyone before. I did not denounce for pleasure (427).

The old waiter's admirable commitment to the *causa*, as he says, and his high introspection visibly transforms the narrator from his firm apolitical, noncommittal stand to an identification with the people's cause. Although the narrator leaves the bar hurriedly before the police arrive to arrest the man, he passes through a horrible phase of conflict that brings out a dramatic change in him finally. He quits the place obviously to keep his hands clean of the matter, but reaching his hotel finds himself in a deadly conflict. He is not able to get over the conflict by any means and, in the end, calls up the secret police head quarters:

"Tell him I denounced him . . . " thus speaks the narrator and resolves his conflict dramatically. Then we hear: "as I walked up the stairs now, I felt much better" (428).

This story has much to contribute to the growth and transformation of the writer's approach to life and has a significant role to play in bringing about a big change in his major works following the Spanish Civil War. First, it shows the writer's hitherto apolitical, noncommittal and isolationist stand that dramatically gave way to a total commitment to and identification with the cause of the Spanish Republic. This process continues through the novel, *For Whom the Bell Tolls*, in which the theme is based on human solidarity: "No man is an Iland", and finally culminates in the cosmic vision of Santiago in *The Old Man and the Sea.* In *For Whom the Bell Tolls* the protagonist, Robert Jordan, regrets that he is a foreigner.

> That I am a foreigner is not my fault. I would rather have been born here ... (*FWBT*, 15).

The next story of this series that is set in the Chicote's against the same tension-ridden atmosphere of Madrid is "The Butterfly and the Tank". It was first published in the *Esquire* in its December issue of 1938. This story is comparatively more tragic than the previous one as it concerns the brutal killing of a highly innocent and well-meaning civilian with plenty of jest and good humor, particularly in a period when the mood was generally dark and tempers short. The story is based on a symbol ("The Butterfly and the Tank") that finally makes the whole issue clear and poignant in its perspective.

This story too, set in Chicote's, begins with a sickly winter shower. The rain itself occasions the story as the narrator is forced into the bar to wait out the rain. Yet another instance of rain as an ominous bringer of misfortune and tragedy in the Hemingway world. The mood in general and the atmosphere corresponds to this sickly winter shower in the war-torn city. The narrator himself sets the mood of the time thus:

> It was the second winter at shelling in the siege of Madrid and everything was short including tobacco and people's tempers and you were a little hungry all the time and would become suddenly and unreasonably irritated at things you could do nothing about, such as the weather (Moscow ed., 314).

It was on such a gloomy, irritating evening that the man got into the bar with a flit gun loaded with eau de cologne. He was one of the very few civilians present in the bar packed with the uniformed people of the militias.

He started his fun by squirting one of the waiters with the flit gun. The waiter was of course quite indignant about it and gave a note of protest. But the man wouldn't stop. Some uniformed militia people got up and threw him out of the bar. But unfortunately, the flit gun man did not think of the consequences of his action and broke in once again and resumed his fun. This time the militiamen pushed him between the tables and shot him dead at a close range. The poor man lay dead in a corner on the floor and the killers escaped confidently while the police made a lot of fuss about it and held up the civilians till midnight.

The next day when the narrator went to the bar the whole issue became clear in the course of his talks with the manager and the waiters. They all realized that ''it was really just an unfortunate misunderstanding'' (Moscow ed., 323).

The narrator recalls how the flit gun man lay miserably on the floor with his shirt ripped open without any undershirt and with a pair of worn out shoes. And the manager adds how his wife came and mourned bitterly over the body until she was taken away by the soldiers. She dropped down by him crying: "Pedro, what have they done to thee, Pedro? Who has done this to thee? Oh, Pedro'' (323).

The tragedy of Pedro, as the manager of the bar suggested to the narrator, was a sort of metaphor that he expressed through ''a butterfly and the tank''. The very act of killing the poor civilian, the smooth escape of the killers, and the very nightmarish, chaotic atmosphere of the time with bombings, shellings and casualty every moment tend to make Pedro's death appear comical.

The individual, as such, was as fragile and as insignificant in that atmosphere as a butterfly would be in the face of a tank.

Commenting on the title and its irony Charles Molesworth comments:

> . . . the misunderstood gaiety coming in contact with the deadly seriousness that is here always (87).

If we recall the writer's story, "The Killers," and compare Nick Adams, its protagonist, with the narrator here, the issue appears clearer. In "The Killers," the predicament of Ole Anderson appeared so much grave and a matter of the utmost concern for Nick while here, the death of Pedro in much more tragic and senseless circumstances does not affect the narrator correspondingly. The endurance that we observe in the narrator of "The Butterfly and the Tank" has possibly grown out of the protagonist's recurring encounter with the sinister forces of the world. Particularly, the violence and horror that was let loose in the wake of the Spanish Civil War acted therapeutically to counteract the trauma that the First World War wound had left in him. That explains why the narrator here does not feel thwarted and vulnerable as Nick Adams and Frederic Henry felt previously. This shows the consolidation of the disturbed, unsettled psyche of the early protagonists and thus anticipates Robert Jordan and Santiago in the days to come.

Finally, the story anticipates *For Whom the Bell Tolls* in its objective treatment of the Loyalist follies. The uniformed militiamen who gunned down the innocent carpenter Pedro and deprived his wife and children of their husband and father were the Republicans, the people's militias, and not the Fascists. Hemingway, throughout his writings, never discriminates between the Fascists and the Loyalists. That is one of the reasons why he was subject to some scathing criticism by the anarchists and the Marxists (Like Alvah Bessie, Arturo Barea, etc.)

The third story of this series, "Night Before Battle", which was published in the February issue of *Esquire* in 1939, is set in the Chicote's mostly. This story gives a realistic picture of the state of affairs during the advanced months of the Civil War when the Loyalists were mostly on their defense and were losing their ground steadily. Ineffective organization, lack of proper planning and inadequate supply of arms were the major reasons for the fall of the Republican resistance. This story gives a glimpse of the whole set up and the prevailing atmosphere of the time. As AL Wagner, the tanker, one of the characters of the story, remarks with disgust: "I don't mind dying a bit. Dying is just a lot of crap. Only it's wasteful" (*Comp. S. Stories*, 443).

The reaction of the tanker is not a sign of his cowardice or his fear of death. It is against the gross mismanagement, disorganization and total absence of planning that he is reacting. Presently they have reached a point when the death of an individual does not serve any purpose. It is simply "wasteful", as he says rightly. His views directly anticipate the dialogue between Gen. Golz and Robert Jordan at the beginning of the book (*FWBT*, 5).

The story concerns three characters; a tanker who fought that day and shall be fighting the next day too, a pilot who has survived a burial in a bombardment, and the narrator himself. They sit in Chicote's and then move into the narrator's room in Hotel Florida and try to spend the night, that seems too long and endless, playing cards and gambling. The atmosphere, in spite of the bright electric lights and activity, has a smell of disaster and death about it. The tanker AL Wagner does most of the talking with the narrator and his voice brings out the whole atmosphere of the night. He refers to their assault next day on the church of the hill. He complains how they "haven't got enough artillery to give any kind of real covering fire to keep them down". Besides, they have to fight in such an ill-equipped manner against a powerful and well-equipped enemy. So he feels strongly that "It's going to be murder" (*Comp. S. Stories*, 441-42).

In a war, when both the armies are not more or less matched in their weapons or artillery, it really becomes a senseless, wasteful murder of individuals. And that is what the story precisely conveys with a small fragment of the Loyalist forces pitted against a far superior rival force toward the end of the Civil War. This anticipates the dreadful night of the cave of Pablo where Robert Jordan lay waiting for the next day's blowing of the bridge. Like Pilar smelling the odour of death in Jordan's hands, AL Wagner, the tanker, feels it himself. He is almost convinced about his imminent death in the next day's assault. So, before they sleep, AL hands over an envelope to the narrator to be sent to his brother in New York. And he retires wishing to meet the narrator in the Chicote's the next night. But when the narrator wants to know at what time, he dismisses him telling: "Listen, that's enough", he said, "Tomorrow night at Chicote's, We don't have to go into the time. And he went out" (459).

The tanker, AL Wagner, puts us in mind of Robert Jordan in *For Whom the Bell Tolls* with his preparedness and courage to die. But Jordan goes a step higher in his manner of acceptance of the reality. He never reacts though the circumstances in which he operates are no better than AL Wagner's.

"All you need is a perspective" (458). AL Wagner says and finally calms down when he gets it. And Robert Jordan never seems to have lost the "perspective"any moment in his brief life. So he maintained his poise and equanimity throughout, though he was directly exposed to death all along.

The last two stories on the Spanish Civil War background, "No Body Ever Dies" and "Under the Ridge", were published in the *Cosmopolitan* in its March and October issues of 1939 respectively. The first one "No Body Ever Dies" is considered to be the weakest of this group for its tone of open propaganda, without any conviction or practical philosophy. Therefore it lacks in realism and literally gets lost in vague idealism and romantic adventurism.

The theme is based on the life and adventures of Enrique, the protagonist, who has just returned to Cuba from fifteen months of fighting in Spain. There is a parallel political struggle in Cuba against the same Fascist forces as in Spain. Enrique is led by his friends to a house where he spends the last few hours of his life with his girl Maria. The house is then raided, Enrique is killed by the police and Maria is taken into police custody.

The story, as such, marginally anticipates the last few hours of Jordan with Maria in Pablo's camp and the tragic separation of the two lovers thereafter in *For Whom the Bell Tolls*. The stoic posture of Maria, the girl in this story, to some extent, resembles that of Jordan's girl in the novel.

The story presents the last few hours of the two lovers' lives before the boy dies. In the course of their talk the boy Enrique tells Maria:

> There are no foreign countries, Maria . . . . Where you die does not matter, if you die for liberty (*Comp. S. Stories*, 475).

The words of Enrique anticipate Robert Jordan. Like the tanker, AL Wagner, in the story, "Night Before Battle", Enrique too complains about the inadequate artillery coverage and the force that was insufficient which, in fact, led to the tragic deaths of a number of young volunteers including Vicente, the brother of the girl.

Besides, the few moments when the two lovers become one in ecstasy anticipate the sleeping bag scene of *For Whom the Bell Tolls.* As they lose themselves in the darkness of the room:

> Then, in the dark on the bed, holding himself carefully, his eyes closed, their lips against each other, the happiness there with no pain, the being home suddenly there with no pain . . . the comfort of being loved and still no pain . . . (477).

They were jerked out of their ecstasy by the sharp, piercing police siren and Enrique soon fell a prey to the police bullets and Maria was taken away into the police custody.

The last story of this group "Under the Ridge" is the most realistic and the best one of this lot. It is because this story gives a realistic and objective picture of the Loyalist operation in the Civil War and shows the causes for its eventual defeat. At the same time, it seems to be partly a continuation of some major strain of *A Farewell to Arms*, while it clearly points to the next novel *For Whom the Bell Tolls*.

The maturity of the vision of the artist which is reflected in this story is mainly due to the sum total of experience that the writer put into it after his four extended visits to Spain, and his first hand experience of the state of affairs during the course of the struggle. This story was published in the October issue of the *Cosmopolitan* in 1939, after Hemingway finally left Spain disheartened seeing no hope for the Loyalists.

The writer, with all his direct experience and wisdom, accumulated through months of painful association with the Republican cause, effectively introduces a character as his spokesman. He is a young Spanish soldier, who knows no fear and has a terribly blunt manner. The dialogue between the narrator and this young Spanish soldier is the focal point of the story. The narrator, though he seems to get shocked at the beginning by the bluntness of the young Spaniard, encourages him all through the conversation and admires his straightforward, unadulterated approach to things.

This young Spaniard is from Extremadura. He has as much pride in introducing himself as an Extremaduran as he has contempt for the foreigners, the Russians in particular. The narrator asks the young Extremaduran in the same way as in "The Old Man at the Bridge":

> "What are your politics?"

"I hate all foreigners; the Moors, the English, the French, the Italians, the Germans, the North Americans and the Russians." But he hates "the Russians most" (462).

> "Are you a Fascist?" asks the narrator. "No," says the man. "I am an Extremaduran and I hate Foreigners" (462).

This part of the conversation between the narrator and the Extremaduran sets the mood of the story and largely suggests the deeper implication of the issue. Why is this Spaniard so bitter about the foreigners, and the Russians in particular, when they come voluntarily to help them fight against the Fascists? Is he crazy? No, the issue is serious and of great consequence. In the course of his talk, he painfully reminisces the long tortuous past of his country. In a voice, charged with emotion, he says:

> I am from Badajoz. In Badajoz, we have been sacked and pillaged and our women violated by the English, the French, now the Moors.

And about why he hates the Russians he says: "Because they are the representatives of tyranny and I hate their faces" (464).

Against this background the story presents two live examples of the diabolical conduct of the Russians in the name of discipline. The first is the case of a French man in the international Brigade who walked out of the line, seeing the hopelessness and stupidity of the attack against an unequal enemy. He was promptly rounded up by two Russians in leather coats and was shot on the very spot from where he had deserted. The second is the case of a boy called Paco who was frightened during the bombardment and shot himself in the hands to get away from the front. But, after he was cured in the hospital the same leather-coat Russians brought him over to the same spot where he had wounded himself, and coolly shot him in the back of his head. "He had no warning and no chance to prepare himself"(467)—these two cases show a continuation of the attempted "separate peace" and the ultimate sway of the sinister forces in the world of *A Farewell to Arms*:

> When such people with the leather-coats and pistols come it is always a bad omen, thus says the young Extremaduran (*Comp. S. Stories*, 467).

The sinister symbol of "The leather-coats" in the Spanish Civil War assumes the manifestation of "Thought Police" in Orwell's *1984*.

This story unveils the long drawn mask on the Russian hypocrisy and double-dealing in the course of the Spanish Civil War that becomes the central issue of the novel, *For Whom the Bell Tolls*. The inadequate supply of arms and artillery, lack of proper planning and coordination and, above all, the brutal and high-handed dealings in the name of discipline made the Fascist victory smooth and easy. Finally, the writer quite effectively brings out the hypocrisy and illusion of the whole thing by showing the tanks in their trail of retreat as victory march on the celluloid. He sums up:

> On the screen they advanced over the hill irresistibly, mounting the crests like great ships, to crawl clanking on toward the illusion of victory (*Comp. S. Stories*, 469).

VI

In a recent book, *The True Gen,* Denis Brian recalls that six days before Franco's men entered Madrid, Hemingway was back home in Key West starting his novel, *For Whom the Bell Tolls*. Brian refers to a letter that Hemingway wrote during this period to Max Perkins in which he said that, now that he was back in America, as a writer his only allegiance was to the truth (121). This declaration of Hemingway, in the context of his novel, *For Whom the Bell Tolls*, is widely acknowledged as genuine and honest. The book, as such, marks the culmination of Hemingway's literary response to the Spanish Civil War. *For Whom the Bell Tolls* is the direct outcome of the writer's commitment to the cause of the Spanish people in their historic Civil War. The novel is based on the theme of the blowing up of a strategic bridge by an American Volunteer dynamiter with the help of a group of Spanish Guerrillas. The entire action centers around the bridge in a rugged Spanish mountain range just below the Fascist line, and the duration of the whole action is only seventy-two hours from the time the protagonist arrives in the guerrilla camp till the bridge is blown, the guerrilla band escapes, and the protagonist dies. Hemingway shows wonderful precision and subtlety in handling the plot and achieves "the true union of passion and reason" that elevates this piece to "a work of art" (Robert Sherwood, 325).

For Whom the Bell Tolls is significant for two main reasons. Firstly, it marks Hemingway's break with his earlier, pre-Spanish Civil War writings, as there is a new theme and a new type of protagonist altogether in this novel. Secondly, the novel also shows a corresponding change in the technique and style of the writer from his earlier writings.

Hemingway shows a consumming interest in violence and death in all his pre-Spanish Civil War novels and stories, including the two non-fiction works which he wrote during the thirties, *Green Hills of Africa* and *Death in the Afternoon*. The theme of violence and death, of course, continues after the Spanish Civil War, but the whole perspective changes. As we see in the *Nick Adams* stories and the first three novels (*SAR, AFTA, THAHN*), the protagonist is invariably an isolated individual struggling desperately, both inside and outside, mentally and physically, against an unequal, hostile, indifferent world. And lastly, the protagonist gets crushed miserably before he finds out the clue, a viable rationale, to justify his struggle. Life, as it were, is subject to the perpetual threat of suffering, violence and death. This is inevitable, not only in Hemingway's writing world, but outside in the world of reality as well.

So, this theme with the inherent human tragedy continues in Hemingway's writing even after the Spanish Civil War. But the fundamental difference that the few later, post-Spanish Civil War novels show is in the transformation of the protagonists' approach to life. While the circumstances or the life as it is, in which the protagonist operates, remains basically the same, these post-Spanish Civil War protagonists show a clear superiority over their predecessors in the very manner of their approach to and acceptance of the reality. What could have brought about such a fundamental change in Hemingway's writing? The first thing that comes to mind is the Spanish ritual of bullfight which fascinated Hemingway greatly and had considerable influence on him. The role of the matador, particularly in administering death to the savage bull in conformity with the strict rules of the ritual, impressed Hemingway greatly. Hemingway took it as a cold defiance of Death, and the manner in which the matador confronts the savage in the arena convinced him as the ultimate standard of courage and endurance on the part of any individual.

Was it then the Spanish bullfight that brought about the change in the later novels like *For Whom the Bell Tolls, Across the River and Into the Trees* and *The Old Man and the Sea*? Critics like Laurence Broer (*The Spanish Tragedy*) have analyzed Hemingway's works in this light.

VII

Here, the stand I have chosen to take is different from that of critics like Broer who try to interpret Hemingway's entire writing in the light of the *Corrida de toros*. The change that sets in *For Whom the Bell Tolls*, in fact, starts from the "death-bed conversion" (Young, 71) of Harry Morgan in *To Have and Have Not*, and the process continues all through the writings of Hemingway, during the Spanish Civil War (such as, *The Spanish Earth, The Fifth Column*, the War Dispatches, and the short stories), till it becomes conspicuous enough in *For Whom the Bell Tolls*.

As we have discussed earlier, Hemingway's protagonists, right from Nick Adams to Harry Morgan, undergo a bitter internal struggle, parallel to their struggle outside with the sinister forces of the world. While Nick Adams is mostly guided by his reflexes, the instinctive, unemotive factors, Jake Barnes, Frederic Henry and Harry Morgan are quite conscious and aware of the conflict inside. So, as it happens in "The Killers", Nick Adams instinctively chooses to run away, without any reflection or analysis of the situation. But the motif, all the same, remains to find out a viable rationale, a meaningful pattern in this inherently tragic frame of life in order to make the struggle for existence tolerable and worthwhile. Nick Adams thus, apparently for his age and immaturity, fails to analyze or articulate his own internal struggle that must be tormenting him. It is Jake Barnes, in *The Sun Also Rises*, who makes the first ever utterance of their quest for the ultimate truth:

> All I wanted to know was how to live in it. May be
> if you found out how to live in it, you learned from
> that what it was all about (*SAR*, 153).

To find a purpose and meaning in this struggle is the ultimate truth that all these protagonists strove for all their life. And finally, it was Harry Morgan who got the enlightenment at the end of his life, when to make any amendment in the light of his realization was not possible any longer. The enlightenment or the regeneration or the realization that Harry Morgan got was subsequently materialized in action by Robert Jordan in *For Whom the Bell Tolls*.

Now the question arises, what ultimately brought about this realization to the dying Harry that continued to illumine the lives of Robert Jordan, Colonel Cantwell and Santiago. It is certainly not the ritual of Spanish bullfight that effected this transformation. Had he been influenced by this ritual, to that extent, he would have written about it long before *To Have and Have Not*. Secondly, had Hemingway been keen on developing his protagonist in the image of the bullfighter he would have preferred not to go for a non-fiction, a treatise on the Spanish bullfight like *Death in the Afternoon*, where he points out its lapses along with its merits. Thirdly, instead of writing the non-fiction and introducing such minor characters like Paco, the boy in the story, "The Capital of the World", or Pedro Romero, the young bullfighter in *The Sun Also Rises*, Hemingway could have introduced full-fledged heroes in his major works.

That the bullfight did not effect the change in the later novels of Hemingway is strongly evidenced from the fact that Hemingway himself could not be free from his fear psychosis or trauma till he went to the Spanish Civil War about which Carlos Baker writes thus:

> Premonitions of possible death struck him periodically like twinges of rheumatism (445).

Baker again writes:

> His first visit to war-time Spain had destroyed his belief in the after-life, but it had also eliminated all his fear of death (481).

Thus, the fear of death that continued to haunt Hemingway was reflected in his early protagonists, along with the attendant complications like insomnia, etc. A point worth noting here is that, in spite of all his exposure to the Spanish bullfight rituals, Hemingway could not get over his chronic fear-psychosis. Even in *Death in the Afternoon* he writes:

> There is no remedy for any thing in life. Death is the sovereign remedy for all misfortunes (104).

He again writes in the same book:

> All stories if continued far enough end in death (122).

This clearly shows that the awareness of Death continues to be his prime concern and, in turn, the supreme controlling factor in Hemingway's life and his writing as well. In both *Death in the Afternoon* and *Green Hills of Africa* we get a clear account of Hemingway's experimentation with bullfighting and big-game hunting, in his own life, visibly to counteract his persisting "trauma". But all these attempts of Hemingway, which were precisely directed towards getting over his own abnormal fear of death, remained incomplete till the Spanish Civil War.

It was during the Spanish Civil War that Hemingway finally succeeds in resolving the life-long conflict that keeps tormenting his protagonists as much as himself. There at last, they realize what they were longing for all their lives. Their quest ends in their identification with the larger mankind that exists beyond their 'self'. They realize the divine touch of human solidarity, of brotherhood and fellow-feeling. And in this process of transformation they get over their narrow individualism, concern for the self and their denial of the larger issues of mankind.

This point becomes clearer when one sets this newly emerging Hemingway protagonist against all his predecessors in the earlier pre-Spanish Civil War works. This new figure, as one sees in Robert Jordan or in Colonel Cantwell or Santiago, shows a clean break with the "lost generation" traits like despair, indecisiveness and sentimentality of their predecessors. They are, on the other hand, bold, decisive, courageous, assertive and confident. And all these changes, so remarkable indeed, could only be possible for their denial of the self and their affiliation to the cause of human solidarity and universal brotherhood. Such commitment to a great cause gives them enough spiritual strength to confront the harsh realities of life, which bullfighting or big-game-hunting could not possibly give. Robert Jordan declares in *For Whom the Bell Tolls*:

> I have fought for what I have believed in . . . if we win here we will win everywhere (*FWBT*, 467).

Jordan continues:

> The world is a fine place and worth fighting for and I hate very much to leave it (*FWBT*, 467).

What Jake Barnes wanted to learn, Robert Jordan has already done. The quest to know the purpose of this struggle, to find a meaning of this perpetual warfare in life, that commences with Nick Adams, finds itself well resolved in Robert Jordan. Thus, as Ivan Kashkeen (1961) justly puts it: "Here, in Spain, Hemingway at last found the right words to be said about victory over death" (167).

Thus the change is conspicuous from Nick Adams to Robert Jordan through Jake Barnes, Frederic Henry and Harry Morgan. The transformation is clear and promising: from *Nada* and nihilism to affirmation, from defeatism to conviction, from despair to optimism and, above all, from self to selflessness, from atomic individualism to social commitment and universal brotherhood. Jordan's complete negation of his own self is manifested in his dedication and commitment to the cause of the Republic. As he ruminates:

> It gave a part in something that you could believe in wholly and completely and in which you felt an absolute brotherhood with the others who were engaged in it. It was something that you have never known before but that you had experienced now and you gave such importance to it and the reasons for it *that your own death seemed of complete unimportance* (*FWBT*, 235) (emphasis mine).

In most of his short stories and early novels Hemingway's protagonist only pursues his own self, his own happiness and security. Either he is totally horrified and baffled as in the case of Nick Adams, or completely confused and rendered helpless like Jake Barnes, or desperately attempting to find out a separate peace away from bombs and bullets like Frederic Henry, or struggling to bring comfort to one's wife and kids like Harry Morgan.

VIII

It is in *For Whom the Bell Tolls*, at last, that the protagonist succeeds in rising above his self and acts for a greater cause. As regards the earlier ones, Paolini (1961) rightly observes that the protagonist is "caught in a deep and unresolved antagonism: The anti-thesis between the "self" and the "anti-self" (132-33).

In *For Whom the Bell Tolls*, thus, the long persisting conflict is finally resolved. This became possible, as Jackson J. Benson believes, owing to Robert Jordan's emotional stability "that can arise only from a strong general faith in humanity" (162). Commenting on the new role that Robert Jordan plays as a Hemingway protagonist in *For Whom the Bell Tolls*, Michael F. Moloney writes that "devotion to any cause outside themselves was something new for the creatures of Hemingway's pen"(190). Yet another critic, Robin H. Farquhar, maintains that Robert Jordan's role is exemplary as he proves that "man may find purpose in life through love for his fellow man" (277). Even Santiago, with his superhuman endurance, composure and control over his situation, does not get so much scope as Robert Jordan to merge in a global brotherhood and to sacrifice his life for the cause ungrudgingly.

Robert Jordan, an American Professor, presently a volunteer dynamiter in the Republican International militia in Spain, is dispatched with orders to blow a strategic bridge across the Fascist line. The blowing of the bridge is carefully scheduled to synchronize with a proposed crackdown on the Fascists. But, from the very beginning, things move unfavorably. Jordan, as per the instruction, is supposed to receive aid and advice from Pablo, a Republican guerrilla leader who camps close to the bridge. But this host of Jordan, who is supposed to help the execution of the plan, goes against the very idea of blowing the bridge and puts his entire weight against Jordan's effort to fulfil the act. And finally, a few hours before the scheduled moment of crackdown, Pablo escapes with the detonators. This is not all that Jordan confronts in executing his assignment. During his three days camp there Jordan gets enough indication that the Fascists have already got the information about their proposed crackdown. In view of this situation the blowing of the bridge, the entire mobilization of the troops and the artillery, would fail to strike its target. So Jordan sends Andres, one of the guerrillas, to the area commander of the Republican army suggesting the calling off of the assault. But his message does not reach its destination owing to gross mismanagement and lack of co-ordination in the Army Head Quarters itself. But, despite all such monstrous handicaps, obstacles and tensions, Jordan finally (as he was instructed) blows up the bridge just at the scheduled hour. As the Republican attack becomes a failure, which Jordan knew much in advance, the Fascists make a prompt counter attack, chasing the guerrillas out of their hideout. Robert Jordan sustains a fatal injury in his leg as his horse falls down on it rendering him immobile. He chooses to stay behind alone to cover the escape of the guerrilla band with his machine-gun till the Fascist infantry arrives.

The action that spread over three days, not only shows, in rare precision, the wholesome personality of a new type of Hemingway protagonist, that Robert Jordan is, but also presents in microcosm the entire gamut of the Spanish Civil War, with all its merits and lapses. In this context, Leo Gurko observes that "the sense of microcosm is worked out exquisitely" (120). Hemingway brilliantly and effectively telescopes the Spanish Civil War of three years duration into three days time. The fight between the Loyalists and the Insurgents (Rebels) has a strong universal note as it represents the perpetual fight that goes on everywhere and everytime in the world between the forces of good and the forces of evil. Similarly, Hemingway realistically presents a cross section of characters, from Pablo and Rafael at one extreme to characters like Anselmo, Jordan and Pilar at the other, representing broadly the evil and the good respectively. The treachery of Pablo, the lack of commitment to the cause in people like Rafael, who chases rabbits when he should guard the entrance, the eccentricity of people at the helm of affairs like Andre Marty, the half-heartedness of General Golz, the double-dealings, the lack of adequate supply of arms and ammunitions by the Russians and, above all, a general mismanagement of things finally led to the Republican failure. On the other hand, foreign volunteers like Robert Jordan, and the native civilians and peasants like Anselmo, Pilar and EL Sordo who fight and sacrifice their lives for the cause, add meaning and justification to the whole struggle. As Williams rightly comments, this set of characters, whom Robert Jordan represents, achieves a "spiritual triumph over material disaster" (141). Arthur Waldhorn observes that, with *For Whom the Bell Tolls* Hemingway breaks a new ground and successfully creates "a promise of transcendence, a unifying and sustaining spirituality that binds not only all Spaniards but all men" (163).

The entire focus of the book is on the bridge which, as Jordan strongly believes, "can be the point on which the future of the human race can turn" (*FWBT*, 43). Thus, the issue is not confined to the Spanish Civil War alone. It is a symbolic presentation of the perpetual struggle going on everywhere in this world, between the good and the evil. People like Jordan rightly realize the issue, in its true perspective, and sustain their commitment till the last. When

Jordan approaches Pablo, the latter tries to demoralize him by dismissing him as a foreigner.

Jordan meets this charge with complete detachment and conviction. He answers:

> If I ask you to help me, you can refuse and I will find others who will help me . . . I have to do what I am ordered to do (15).

Jordan shows his firm commitment to the cause when he says:

> That I am a foreigner is not my fault. I would rather have been born here (15).

The undiluted sincerity and commitment to a cause that Jordan considers to be ideal and worth pursuing shows the depth of his morals and the strength of his personality. Jordan, in this respect, rises far above his predecessors.

The circumstances in which Jordan operates are no less challenging and disappointing than Santiago's. The hostility of Pablo keeps Jordan on tenterhooks all the while, culminating in his shocking act of decamping with the detonators. But, despite all such giant obstacles Jordan carries out his assignment with complete grace and self-control. Again, the affair that he develops with Maria is no less an emotional pressure than any other factor. But he gets over that conflict between duty and love with great ease which is the manifestation of his firm, unwavering commitment to the cause that he is determined to serve at all costs.

After he is fatally wounded in his leg and lies immobile when the Fascist troops are chasing the guerrillas out of their hide-out, Jordan persuades everyone to leave and covers the escape of the group with his machine gun till the Fascists arrive. During that brief period of time Jordan undergoes excruciating pain, and has a bitter conflict in his mind whether to pull the trigger and put an end to his agonizing pain. But he soon restrains himself and says in an internal monologue:

> No, it isn't. Because there is something you can do yet (470).

And he says again:

> And if you wait and hold them up even a little while
> or just get the officer that may make all the difference.
> One thing well done can make—(470).

The above internal monologue gives a clear view of Jordan's mind. The tremendous pressure he is subject to during his stay in Pablo's camp, and finally after he is wounded, till he confronts the Fascist officer and dies, is no less than Santiago's classic struggle with the giant marlin and the pack of killer sharks in the sea. The endurance, the "grace under pressure" and, above all, the clear reasoning that upholds Jordan's commitment to duty can, under no circumstances, be treated as a lesser achievement than Santiago's. Besides, the humility that arises from the negation of the self, that marks Jordan's character from the very beginning till the end, is a clear mark of superiority over all his predecessors. Further, as is evident from these monologues his entire attention is focused on serving the cause of mankind, which Santiago does not have. In his case, there is a great commitment to his duty as a fisherman which is being accentuated by his superhuman endurance. But in Jordan's case, as John M. Muste observes:

> We have for the first time a Hemingway hero who believes that his actions can and will affect the destinies of other men (96).

This new orientation of Hemingway's protagonists, from self to selflessness, from 'I' to 'We', in conformity with his commitment to some greater cause, such as a service to a noble cause (Like Jordan) or simply a high sense of duty (as in Santiago), brings about a drastic change in their attitude to violence. In all the pre-Spanish Civil War writings, as we have seen, violence is accepted "as simply a condition of life and a constant threat to the individual" (Muste, 95). None of the earlier protagonists ever resort to violence before Harry Morgan, who kills one Chinese Mr. Sing, and justifies the killing as necessary to prevent further killings by him. In *For Whom the Bell Tolls* we find that violence and killing are justified on a regular basis, as a creed, in the interest of the larger community.

Robert Jordan strongly believes that violence can be ethical when it is necessary to prevent greater violence, the new trend set by Harry Morgan in *THAHN*. He says:

> No Man has a right to take another man's life unless it is to prevent something worse happening to other people (304).

Thus violence, for the first time in Hemingway's canon, is pressed into the service of the people, of mankind at large. "This is a drastic change", as John M. Muste comments (97). In his life, Robert Jordan fully justifies Donne's meditation that Hemingway chooses as his epigraph, and a part of it as the title of his novel:

> No Man is an iland, intire of itself . . . any man's *death* diminishes *me*, because I am involved in *Mankinde*: and therefore never send to know for whom the *bell* tolls: It tolls for *thee*.

The influence of the Spanish Civil War was enormous and far-reaching on Hemingway's writing. Hemingway's participation in the cause brought about a complete reorientation of his approach to life that was marked by a change in the thematic pattern of his writings as well as style. In fact, with *For Whom the Bell Tolls* a clear departure from Hemingway's previous writings is strongly realized on the point of his narrative technique and style.

IX

The first two novels of Hemingway, *The Sun Also Rises* and *A Farewell to Arms*, are in the first person narrative mode. The autobiographical nature of the two novels and the typical psychology of their protagonists could be effectively communicated through the first person narrative. The success and popularity of these novels was mostly due to the effective use of the first person narrative. The protagonists are out and out self-oriented, withdrawing and complex. Thus, as Halliday observes, the first person narrative technique in the first two novels is quite effective in producing an effect of ''singularity'', in the context of the ''emotional isolation''of the protagonists in the novels' ''theme of moral atrophy'' (175).

The next novel, *To Have and Have Not*, which shows Hemingway's initial break with his previous pattern is a mixture of the first person and third person. To my thinking, it is mainly for the shifting of focus, from 'I' to 'We', from singularity to plurality, in Hemingway's writing. The technical irregularity in *To Have and Have Not*, as pointed out by many critics, is primarily due to the ''confusion of theme'' (Halliday, 180). Nevertheless, the book reflects the transition in Hemingway's approach in general with its corresponding change in the narrative technique.

But this irregularity of technique, owing to a confusion of theme in *To Have and Have Not*, gets completely cleared up in the next novel, *For Whom the Bell Tolls*. Presently we see Hemingway in a very satisfactory position in perfect control of his narrative perspective. Another important point worth noting is that the fumbling transition that starts in *To Have and Have Not* settles down to a farm attitude and world-view in *For Whom the Bell Tolls*.

The protagonist is no more cut off in his own sentimental world. He is no more bothered about his own safety or happiness, for he is now a part of the larger mankind. Hence, there is inevitably a corresponding change in the technique to facilitate an effective communication. As Halliday analyses this point, ''No man is an Iland could not have been adequately presented by means of first person narrative'' (180).

Practically, for a theme like that of *For Whom the Bell Tolls*, where the focus is on human inter-dependence and a global brotherhood, Hemingway very rightly and timely switches over to the omniscient narrative pattern. Thus the narrator is free to move from one character to another and relate the past and the future quite naturally and easily. As Mark Schorer comments on this point:

> In *For Whom the Bell Tolls* we may witness a new style, less brilliant but more flexible, as it integrates itself. That is a very exciting literary spectacle (87).

The effectiveness of Hemingway's changing technique is brilliantly reflected in the two spectacular accounts that Pilar gives in the course of the novel. First, she recalls the first day of the revolution and describes in every detail how the Fascists were taken out one by one, beaten with flails and thrown over a cliff. In her second account, she recalls her life with a bullfighter and the last dinner they shared before he died of consumption. In both the accounts, the psychology of the individuals, with their general as well as particular traits, are presented in a masterly manner in all their subtlety. This again becomes possible owing to the omniscient narrative technique that Hemingway adapts here. In the first account, the psychology of the mob and the horror of human frenzy are portrayed in a life-like manner. Similarly, in her second account, Pilar effectively presents the typical helplessness, the horror and the plight of the bullfighter, Finito, who is dying of consumption when a grand dinner is thrown in his honor. As Pilar narrates:

> Everyone shouted and applauded, and Finito sank further back in the chair and then everyone was quiet and looking at him and he said, No, No, and looked at the bull and pulled further back and then he said, 'No' very loudly and a big blob of blood came out and he didn't even put up a napkin and it slid down his chin.... He looked around at the table and said 'No' once more and then he put the napkin up to his mouth and then he just sat there like that and said nothing and the banquet which had started so well and promised to mark an epoch was not a success (*FWBT*, 188).

Pilar's story is held in very high esteem by many critics. As a very recent critic Edward F. Stanton observes, "Pilar's story recalls unmistakably Goya's *Disasters of War* and to a lesser extent Picasso's *Guernica*" (179).

Besides the effective use of the omniscient narrative perspective, Hemingway makes frequent use of the interior monologue and flashback techniques. Rovit is of the opinion that:

> Hemingway made a fuller dramatic use of the

> memory flashback and of the interior monologue in this novel than in any of his other fictions (140).

Thus we have a considerably greater access to Jordan's past and his thinking processes than any of the earlier Hemingway protagonists or even the later ones. They facilitate the communication of the past and the future, as well as the complex inner workings of the human mind to a great extent. The characterization particularly becomes much more powerful. Carlos Baker acknowledges this aspect when he says: "the principles of characterization-in-depth is strong in *For Whom the Bell Tolls* more so than in any of Hemingway's previous work" (*Writer as Artist*, 250).

Further, Carlos Baker considers this change in *For Whom the Bell Tolls* as "ingestion" from the earlier technique of "suggestion" (*Writer as Artist*, 250).

The previous technique of "suggestion" and understatement give way to "ingestion" in *For Whom the Bell Tolls*. This marks a "bearing within" and an expression of what, as Carlos Baker maintains, "formerly would have been excluded in favor of suggestion" (250).

This shifting from "suggestion" to "ingestion", as Carlos Baker observes, is closely linked to Hemingway's iceberg analogy.

"The larger the visible part of the iceberg," argues Wylder, "the more there is beneath the surface"(131). Thus the point worth noting here is that what Hemingway theorizes in *Death in the Afternoon* is put into practice in *For Whom the Bell Tolls*.

Such change in Hemingway's narrative technique enriches his prose and style considerably. F.I. Carpenter (1961), in a very convincing essay, argues that in *For Whom the Bell Tolls* Hemingway really achieves the "fifth dimension", which he had prophesied in *Green Hills of Africa*.

Hemingway, as Carpenter argues, attains the "fifth dimension" through the intensification of experience in an emotionally charged atmosphere of love or war, "resulting in an ecstasy transcending the traditional limitations of time and of self" (198). On the other hand, contrary to these later works, Hemingway's early works lack this awareness of time and, therefore, fail to experience the ecstasy as their level of experience seemed largely sensational, often ending in a feeling of *Nada*. The telescoping of time and the intensity of experience during Robert Jordan's three days' stay in the guerrilla camp makes the "fifth dimension" possible. As Jordan ruminates:

> May be that is my life and instead of being three score years and ten . . . I suppose it is possible to live as full a life in seventy hours as in seventy years ... (*FWBT*, 166).

Jordan again says to himself:

> "May be I have had all my life in 3 days" (*FWBT*, 355).

Carpenter then points out how Jordan achieves a mystic transcendence of time in the final chapters of the book when, after being wounded, he comforts Maria: "Thou art me too now. Thou art all there will be of me" (464).

"Thus finally," Carpenter says, "The experience of 'the perpetual now' leads to the mystical experience" (198).

This intensity of experience that Jordan achieves in *FWBT* transcends time and achieves a new "value" or "dimension" (199). In this context, Earl Rovit points out that "the suspension of space and time makes it possible for Hemingway to get the effect of always-time" (141).

For Whom the Bell Tolls, thus, is Hemingway's first full-length novel with a new approach to life marked by a new narrative technique and style The critics are unanimous in acknowledging this fact. Howard Mumford Jones, commenting on *FWBT*, says that here "manner has been replaced by style, and the mere author has died out in the artist" (316). Edmund Wilson acknowledges that "*For Whom the Bell Tolls* is a new departure" for Hemingway (320). Robert Sherwood, in his review of this novel, calls it "a work of art" (325). Joseph Warren Beach gives an exhaustive assessment of this novel thus:

> This novel is the largest in scope, the most accomplished in technique and the strongest in effect of anything he has written (69).

Thus with *For Whom the Bell Tolls* we find a clear departure of Hemingway from his earlier writings. This break in the pattern seems to be largely due to Hemingway's changing response to life in general which effected a corresponding change in the narrative technique and style. Now the question arises whether Hemingway's change in his philosophy of life, as this novel after the Civil War shows, is decisive and lasting, or merely a passing phase. The point of serious concern, as such, is whether the admirable stand that Robert Jordan (the new type of protagonist) takes in *For Whom the Bell Tolls* will last or collapse as quickly as it had set in.

X

Hemingway's earlier works are invariably affected by symptoms like nihilism, skepticism, ego and sentimentality which Robert Jordan successfully overcomes. Now, therefore, it should be our major concern to examine whether Hemingway's next novel *Across the River and Into the Trees* really perpetuates the change. This novel would determine whether Hemingway would keep up the new trend set in *For Whom the Bell Tolls.*

It is a fact that this novel *Across the River and Into the Trees*, that came out a decade after the publication of *For Whom the Bell Tolls* , was greatly disappointing as the critics accorded a very cold reception to it. The critics mostly considered this novel as Hemingway's regression to his earlier writings, with its strong autobiographical nature and its obsession with death again.

But all such unfavorable criticism does not seem to dampen the issue that we are concerned with. *Across the River and Into the Trees* may be a partial artistic set back, for its alleged lack of imagination, its autobiographical overtones and its ineffective dialogue. However, we are here primarily concerned with the question whether Hemingway's changing philosophy of life, that commences in the wake of the Spanish Civil War (as *For Whom the Bell Tolls* shows), does really continue through *ARIT*.

To know the truth, we must examine the circumstances in which the protagonist Col. Cantwell operates. Next, we must consider the protagonist's approach to life and the manner in which he confronts the reality.

Colonel Richard Cantwell, the protagonist of the novel *ARIT*, is a fifty-year-old Army officer with a badly damaged heart. He is in love with Renata, a beautiful nineteen years old Venetian girl. When the story begins, we find the old Colonel coming to Venice to see his young mistress and for a duck shoot. Right from the beginning we are made aware of his serious heart condition which he himself is acutely aware of. But, in his action and talk, there is no sign of hopelessness, desperation or weakness. At the age of fifty and with a worn-out heart, he is still capable of loving his teenaged mistress with a rare intensity. Finally, after a very pleasant time in the company of the girl in Venice, he indulges in his favorite sport of shooting ducks, and on his way back to the Army Head Quarters has a fatal stroke and dies consciously, calmly, without any fear or regret. As Wirt Williams very justly comments: "Cantwell resists his catastrophe deliberately, defiantly, even as he knows it is inevitable" (155).

Thus, the predicament of Cantwell, like that of Robert Jordan, is not in any way less disappointing than that of Nick Adams, Jake Barnes, Frederic Henry or Harry Morgan. His world, like Jordan's, is still that of the individual set against an irrational, omnipotent force. But the Colonel, very much like Robert Jordan, achieves a spiritual victory over a material disaster, by confronting it boldly, squarely, right in its face. Col. Cantwell, as far as his approach to life and the basic strength of his personality are concerned, comes closer to Robert Jordan than any of his predecessors. He is bold, positive, decisive and confident. He is courageous, affirmative, free from the touch of nihilism and *Nada*. He is capable of profound love and high seriousness. Moreover, his timely decision to meet his beloved just before his death makes his life purposeful and his death meaningful. At this point, Cantwell's life comes closer to Jordan's. We may recall the fact that soon after Jordan reaches Pablo's camp he knows the impending failure of the Republican offensive. Pilar too reads in his palm the mark of death and gets the smell of death around him.

Nevertheless, Jordan avails himself of those last few hours of his life making love to Maria intensely, and fulfils his commitment to the cause by blowing up the bridge and, finally, dies while covering the escape of his gang from the Fascists. Here, the point worth noting is that the knowledge of impending death, for Cantwell and Jordan as well, does not make any difference in their life and commitment to things. They remain unperturbed, calm and poised till the very last. And particularly, for their intensity of love, they attain an ecstasy that helps them transcend their fear of death.

Col. Cantwell comes closer to Jordan thus on three main points. First, he does not face an abrupt, violent death like Catherine or Harry Margan. Second, he knows for certain about the condition of his heart that refuses to serve him long. Yet he maintains his virility, his "old Wild-boar truculence"(*ARIT*, 71). He says calmly: "I know where I'm going"(*ARIT*, 252).

Never for a moment does Cantwell resign himself to a state of *Nada* or despondency. Nor does he ever make any attempt to seek a separate peace. On this very point, he is quite different from the earlier protagonists and much closer to the later protagonists like Jordan and Santiago.

On another point, *Across the River and Into the Trees* seems to be a continuation of *For Whom the Bell Tolls*. Like Jordan, Cantwell has no regret, no complaint about anything in life. He is highly positive in his approach and detached to a great extent.

Thirdly, he is a soldier like Jordan, used to discipline and team-works, and *Across the River and Into the Trees* is full of the Colonel's reminiscences of the war. He says:

> "I'm a lucky son of a bitch and I should never be sad about anything" (*ARIT*, 254).

At this point he exactly echoes Jordan who says:

> "You have had much luck" (*FWBT*, 466).

Another point that shows the continuity of *Across the River and Into the Trees* from *For Whom the Bell Tolls* is the consummation of Cantwell's love for Renata. The ecstasy he experiences in his love for Renata is itself transcendental, a spiritual triumph over the biological force that threatens the old Colonel. In one of the intimate love scenes, in chapter XXVIII, Col. Cantwell kisses her and embraces her during which "he only thought of her and how she felt and how close life comes to death when there is ecstasy" (219). "This radical intensification of experience" is described by F.I. Carpenter (1961) as the attainment of the "fifth dimension" in prose in the context of *For Whom the Bell Tolls* (196).

Again, both for Jordan and for Cantwell, "Death" means no horror, unlike in the case of their predecessors. As Cantwell says:

> I have lived with it nearly all my life and the disposing of it has been my trade (*ARIT*, 220).

Death is no stranger to Cantwell. He has literally lived with Death almost all his life and he has no fear or anxiety. This experience particularly was the life-long quest or struggle for the Hemingway protagonist till Harry Morgan. It was during the brief moments of his life before death that Harry succeeds in realizing the truth, the secret of conquering it. And that triumph over death, the fear of death rather, is the speciality with *For Whom the Bell Tolls* and *Across the River and Into the Trees* as well. In view of this, *Across the River and Into the Trees*, with all its congenital limitations, is never a step backward. It is, on the other hand, a clear step forward from *For Whom the Bell Tolls* to *The Old Man and the Sea.*

Across the River and Into the Trees is replete with evidences that prove the strong positive attitude of Cantwell, very much in the manner of Robert Jordan and Santiago. Cantwell, in one of his interior monologues, addresses Death:

> But you can sheath your scythe, old brother death if you have got a sheath for it (*ARIT*, 254).

Here Cantwell almost echoes Santiago's challenge to the sharks and his welcome to the giant marlin to a fair fight.

Like Santiago again who loves the great fish who literally drags him out of life, Cantwell loves his enemies. When Renata asks Cantwell about Rommel:

> "Did you really like Rommel?"
>
> "Very much."

> "But he was your enemy."
>
> "I love enemies, sometimes, more than my friends" (286).

The above attitude of Cantwell shows his strength of personality, his broadness of heart and his heroic spirit. At this point Cantwell comes very close to Santiago, Jordan and Anselmo, the old guerrilla with Jordan, who stands by him till he dies. By their love for the enemy, they show their firm affiliation to the larger mankind, to the universal brotherhood. To reach such spiritual heights one must rise far above one's own petty self.

Wylder makes the following observation on Cantwell:

> He is not, like Jake Barnes or Frederic Henry, the man things happen to, with the exception of that one thing that happens to every man, death, which was denied to both Barnes and Harry within the confines of the novel (169).

Finally, when Cantwell dies, he shows his great detachment, endurance and poise. The moment he senses the stroke he calmly (even in death-pain) comes to the back seat of the car, shuts the door and lies flat, closing all the pages of his life for good.

Thus we can conclude that, despite all the apparent limitations of *Across the River and Into the Trees*, it still keeps the new trend moving. Besides maintaining a "consciously developed style" (*Oppel*, 225) this book once again shows the spiritual transcendence that Hemingway's protagonist achieves through his sublimation of ego. Therefore, the trend that begins with *For Whom the Bell Tolls* continues in *Across the River and Into the Trees* and *The Old Man and the Sea.*

XI

As it becomes clear from our preceding discussion, all the protagonists of Hemingway, from Nick Adams to Colonel Richard Cantwell, move in a world that is basically the same, where the lone individual fights with an unequal, hostile world around. But the fundamental difference between the post-Spanish Civil War writings and the pre-Spanish Civil War writings lies in "the perspective". While all the earlier Hemingway protagonists, from Nick Adams to Frederic Henry, struggle all their lives just to get "a perspective", the later ones since Harry Morgan continue to have the "perspective" all along. We may recall AL Wagner, the tankman in Hemingway's Spanish Civil War short story "Night Before Battle", who knew very well that their next day's offensive would be disastrous. Yet he longs just for "a perspective" to gain emotional stability in the face of such a frustrating and frightening circumstance. What AL Wagner calls "a perspective" we call in several other ways like "purpose", "meaning" or "rationale". In fact, what subtly differentiates the later protagonists from the earlier ones is their hold on the "perspective", which Harry Morgan attains before he dies.

This "perspective" is what Nick Adams unconsciously longs for, Jake Barnes searches all his life, and Frederic Henry does not get till the last. And finally, their life-long quest comes to an end when the flash of illumination comes to Harry Morgan at last. From this point, therefore, there is a drastic change in the Hemingway-protagonist's approach to life in general, with the marks becoming more and more conspicuous till it reaches a point of culmination in *The Old Man and the Sea.*

The process of transformation that commences with Harry Morgan's death is complete with Santiago in *The Old Man and The Sea*. In Philip Rawlings (*The Fifth Column*), we see the first mark of change with his liberation from the cramping effects of the hitherto centralized self. The manner in which Philip resolves the conflict between love and duty, in conformity with his strong commitment to a nobler cause, shows clearly the changing response of the Hemingway-protagonist. In the next major work, *For Whom the Bell Tolls*, the change assumes a clear and concrete shape. Robert Jordan, its protagonist, along with some of the minor characters like the old guerrilla, Anselmo, Pilar, EL Sordo and Maria, firmly establishes the newly shifted focus from an isolated individualism to the theme of human solidarity and interdependence, as powerfully suggested through Donne's Meditation: "No man is an Iland".

The strongest point that all these three post-Spanish Civil War protagonists of Hemingway (Jordan, Cantwell and Santiago) share is their "resoluteness". Each of them finds himself in a greatly disappointing and helpless situation, but with his resoluteness he stands up against all odds, and finally attains a moral transcendence over misfortune and death.

Another aspect worth noting about these three later protagonists is the telescoping of time. In the case of Robert Jordan, his whole life is intensely realized in three days time. Cantwell avails himself of the few days left in his life with his girl and tries to live a complete life before he dies. Santiago struggles with the marlin and then with sharks on the sea for three days and learns what he had not learnt in his whole life.

XII

Compared to Robert Jordan and Cantwell Santiago's realizations in life are much more mature and extensive in scope. While Jordan saw an inherent fraternity in the whole of mankind and was thus committed to it, Santiago's vision of life is much larger, more complex.

The old man's feelings and concerns are not monopolized by the homo-sapiens alone. They are shared by the fish, the birds, the turtles, and the distant stars as well. Thus the old man's sphere is much larger than Jordan's, with his cosmic vision of life as against the global in the case of the latter.

The sad plight of the sea-turtle draws the old man's attention when he finds them mercilessly butchered by people while their hearts keep beating still. The old man promptly identifies himself with the creature and thinks, "I have such a heart too and my feet and hands are like theirs"(*OMAS*, 34).

Then Santiago welcomes the little warbler and says in a tone full of love and concern:

> "Take a good rest, small bird," he said. "Then go

> in and take your chance like any man or bird or fish" (*OMAS*, 53).

In fact, here lies the very crux of the old man's philosophy of life. The old man, with his long experience from the struggle in life, perceives the bond underlying all the creatures in the world, who share the same capricious, violent life. It could be the little delicate warbler or the giant imposing marlin or the deadly scavenger sharks. As Laurence Broer observes, the old man feels in them a "primal relationship—the relationship of the hunter and the hunted" (105). This realization determines the old man's life and thoughts all along. He tells the marlin:

> I love you and respect you very much. But I will kill you dead before this day ends (*OMAS*, 52).

He loves the fish and respects it. Yet he has no compunction to kill it. He is very clear in his reason and thus the conflict between emotion and duty does not bother him.

He knows that he is a fisherman and it is his duty to kill the fish. He strongly believes, "I am as clear as the stars that are my brothers" (*OMAS*, 76). Similarly, he kills the dentuso and justifies the act thus: "I killed him in self-defense" (*OMAS*, 105). This justification of violence is yet another trait of the post-Spanish Civil War novels of Hemingway. Santiago's stand here is very close to Jordan's who too believed that taking another one's life is not wrong "if it is to prevent something worse happening to other people" (*FWBT*, 304). Santiago goes a step further with his perception of the subtle unity in this vast and varied world where "everything kills everything else in some way" (*OMAS*, 106).

As the old man reflects further, "fishing kills me exactly as it keeps me alive"(*OMAS*, 106), and identifies completely with the fish, the bird and the turtle, who are in the same existential struggle for survival. In such a world where to kill or to get killed is the underlying principle, Santiago, as Leo Gurko believes, finds "a unity and emotion which transcends the destructive pattern" in which everyone is caught (162).

Thus the old man is completely free from the complexes and negative traits that the earlier characters like Nick, Jake and Henry have. The open and positive nature of Santiago's character is clearly reflected in his sportive challenge to the fish:

> Come on and kill me. I do not care who kills who (*OMAS*, 92).

This is the loftiest realization one may aspire to have in the struggle of life. This knowledge not only develops one's acceptance of things, it brings in a tremendous feeling of detachment that acts as a powerful antidote to do away with the fear of death and make one really liberated. This knowledge precisely differentiates a Santiago from a Nick Adams or a Frederic Henry. Even Robert Jordan does not have this knowledge the way Santiago has it. This explains the clarity and boldness that feature Santiago's assertion. At a single point, however, Jordan closely anticipates Santiago when he realizes:

> Neither you nor this old man is anything, you are instruments to do your duty (*FWBT*, 43).

Another aspect which Santiago's personality reveals is his humility that he acquires in the course of his ordeal on the sea. It grows as a part of his increasing introspection, yet another mark of improvement on Robert Jordan. First Santiago realizes it in the context of the marlin: "Man is not much beside the great birds and beasts" (*OMAS*, 67).

Presently Santiago realizes that "It was not disgraceful and it carried no loss of true pride" to have humility (110). The old man soon acknowledges the human interdependence when he thinks:

> The boy keeps me alive, he thought. I must not deceive myself (106).

And from this humility comes his further realizations. Now the whole perspective becomes clear to him. Besides the boy Manolin, he now remembers all his good neighbors who must be worrying for him, and he realizes "I live in a good town"(115). This shows his ultimate identification with mankind. And it proves the inappropriateness of Leo Gurko's comment that "*The Old Man and the Sea* is the culmination of Hemingway's . . . disengagement from the social world" (171). In the end, when he reaches his shack and the boy comes to him, he immediately realizes "how pleasant it was to have someone to talk to instead of speaking only to himself and to the sea" (125).

Similarly, when Santiago sees flying fish in the sea he regards them as his "principal friends in the ocean" (26). And when he sees a flight of wild ducks, the old man thinks "No man was ever alone on the sea" (*OMAS*, 59). This shows the continuation of the theme of "No man is an Iland".

This feeling is further reinforced when the sharks fall upon the fish and tear it to pieces. The old man feels unbearable pain when he says:

> I should not have gone out so far, fish, he said. Neither for you nor for me. I'm sorry fish (110).

And, in the course of his introspection, Santiago realizes:

> You violated your luck when you went too far outside (117).

His suspicion now becomes confirmed that his misfortune is due to his going "far out", "beyond all people in the world", where the marlin had rightfully chosen to be "beyond all snares and traps and treacheries" (48).

This human solidarity and interdependence gives meaning and adds purpose to the otherwise existential struggle in life. Previously, the earlier protagonists could not see beyond themselves and, therefore, could not experience the larger life which the later protagonists get plentifully. In spite of all their misfortunes and tragedy, these later characters could still maintain a positive, highly affirmative view of life. Santiago, after the terrible ordeals on the sea, still could say, "I live in a good town"; Robert Jordan too has no regret for all the misfortune and tragedy that befall him; Cantwell, on the threshold of death, still considers himself a "lucky son of a bitch" (*ARIT*, 254).

Santiago expresses this affirmative attitude thus:

> "But man is not made for defeat," he said. "A man can be destroyed but not defeated" (103).

WORKS CITED

Baker, Carlos. *Hemingway: A Life Story*. Penguin. 1989.

Baker, Carlos. *The Writer as Artist*. Princenton. N.J.: Princeton University Press, 1952.

Beach, Joseph Warren. *American Fiction: 1920-1940*. New York: Russell, 1960.

Benson, Jackson J. *Hemingway: The Writers' Art of Self Defence*. Minneapolis: University of Minnesota Press, 1969.

Brian, Denis. *The True Gen*. New York: Grove Press, 1988.

Broer, Laurence R. *Hemingway's Spanish Tragedy*. Alabama: University of Alabama Press, 1973.

Brooks, Atkinson. *Hemingway: The Critical Heritage*, ed. Jeffrey Meyers. London, Boston and Henley: Routledge and Kegan Paul, 1982.

Burgum Edwin Berry. "Review of *The Fifth Column and the First Forty-nine Stories*" *New Masses* 9 (November 22, 1939): 21.

Capellan, Angel. *The Hispanic World*. Michigan: UMI Research Press, 1985.

Carpenter, F.I. "Hemingway Achieves the Fifth Dimension." In *Hemingway and His Critics*, ed. Carlos Baker. New York: Hill and Wang, 1961.

Coleman, Arthur. "Hemingway's Spanish Earth." *Hemingway Review* 2.1 (Fall 1982): 64-67.

Cooper, Stephen. *The Politics of Ernest Hemingway*. Michigan: UMI Research Press, 1987.

Farquhar, Robin H. "Dramatic Structure in the Novels of Ernest Hemingway." *Modern Fiction Studies* 14.3 (Autumn 1968): 271-82.

Fellner, Harriet. *Hemingway as Playwright: The Fifth Column*. Michigan: UMI Research Press, 1986.

Gurco, Leo. *Ernest Hemingway: And the Pursuit of Heroism*. New York: Thomas Y. Crowell, 1968.

Halliday, E.M. "Hemingway's Narrative Perspective," *Ernest Hemingway: Critiques of Four Major Novels*, ed. Carlos Baker. New York: Scribners, 1962. 174-182.

Hemingway, Ernest. "The Butterfly and the Tank." *Selected Short Stories by Ernest Hemingway*. Moscow: Progress Publishers, 1971.

Hemingway, Ernest. "The Night Before Battle." *Complete Short Stories*. New York: Scribners, 1987.

Hemingway, Ernest. "No Body Ever Dies." *Complete Short Stories*. New York: Scribners, 1987.

Hemingway, Ernest. "Under the Ridge." *Complete Short Stories*. New York: Scribners, 1987.

Hemingway, Ernest. "The old Man at the Bridge." *Selected Short Stories* by Ernest Hemingway. Moscow: Progress Publishers, 1971.

Jones, Howard Mumford. *Hemingway: The Critical Heritage*, ed. Jeffrey Meyers. London, Boston and Henley: Routledge and Kegan Paul, 1982.

Kashkeen, Ivan. "Alive in the Midst of Death: Ernest Hemingway." *Hemingway and His Critics*, ed. Carlos Baker. New York: Hill and Wang, 1961.

Letters of F. Scott Fitzgerald, ed. Andrew Turnbull. New York: Scribners, 1963.

Molesworth, Charles. "Hemingway's Code: The Spanish Civil War and World Power." *Salmagundi* 76-77 (Fall 1987-Winter 1988) :84-100.

Moloney, Michael. "Ernest Hemingway:The Missing Third Dimension." In *Hemingway and His Critics*, ed. Carlos Baker. New York: Hill and Wang, 1961. 180-191.

Muste, John M. *Say That We Saw Spain Die*. Seattle and London: University of Washington Press, 1966.

Nakjavani, Erik. "Intellectuals as Militants: Hemingway's *For Whom the Bell Tolls*. and Malraux's *L'espoir*: A Comparative Study." *Rewriting the Good Fight*, eds. Frieda S. Brown, et al.

East Lansing, Michigan: Michigan University Press, 1989. 199-214. *NANA* Dispatches. *Hemingway Review*. Special Number. 7.2 (Spring 1988).

Oppel, Forst. Hemingway's "*Across the River and Into the Trees*". *Hemingway and His Critics*, ed. Carlos Baker. New York: Hill and Wang, 1961. 213-226.

Paolini, Pier Francesco. "The Hemingway of the Major Works." *Hemingway and His Critics*, ed. Carlos Baker. New York: Hill and Wang, 1961. 131-144.

Philips, Gene D. *Hemingway and Film*. New York: Frederick Ungar Pub. Co., 1980.

Schorer, Mark. "The Back-ground of a Style." *Ernest Hemingway: Critiques of Four Major Novels*, ed. Carlos Baker. New York: Scribners, 1962. 87-94.

Sherwood, Robert. *Hemingway: The Critical Heritage*, ed. Jeffrey Meyers. London, Boston and Henley: Routledge and Kegan Paul, 1982.

Smith Julian. "Christ Times Four: Hemingway's Unknown Spanish Civil War Stories." *Arizona Quarterly* 25.1 (Spring 1969): 5-16.

Stanton, Edward F. *Hemingway and Spain: A Pursuit*. University of Washington Press, 1989.

Tanner, Stephen L. The Price of Duty in Hemingway's "*The Fifth Column*", Paper presented in the Spanish Civil War Conference at the University of Brussels in October 1986.

Thomas, Hugh. *The Spanish Civil War*. New York: Harper, 1961.

Waldhorn, Arthur. *A Reader's Guide to Ernest Hemingway*. New York: Farrar, Straus and Giroux, 1972.

Williams, Wirt. *The Tragic Art of Ernest Hemingway*. London: Louisiana State University Press, 1981.

White, William. *By-Line: Ernest Hemingway*. New York: Scribners, 1967.

Wilson, Edmund. *Hemingway: The Critical Heritage*, ed. Jeffrey, Meyers. London, Boston and Henley: Routledge and Kegan Paul, 1982.

Wood Jasper. *Introduction to the Spanish Earth* by Ernest Hemingway. Cleveland: Savage, 1938.

Wylder, Delbert E. *Hemingway's Heroes*. University of Mexico Press, 1969.

Index